THE
HOLY SPIRIT
IN THE NEW
TESTAMENT

General Editors
Core Biblical Studies
Louis Stulman, *Old Testament*
Warren Carter, *New Testament*

Other Books in the Core Biblical Studies Series
The Apocrypha by David A. deSilva
The Dead Sea Scrolls by Peter Flint
Apocalyptic Literature in the New Testament by Greg Carey
God in the New Testament by Warren Carter
Christology in the New Testament by David L. Bartlett
John and the Johannine Letters by Colleen M. Conway
The Pentateuch by Marvin A. Sweeney

CORE BIBLICAL STUDIES

THE
HOLY SPIRIT
IN THE NEW
TESTAMENT

JOHN T. CARROLL

Abingdon Press™

Nashville

THE HOLY SPIRIT IN THE NEW TESTAMENT
Copyright © 2018 by Abingdon Press

This book is printed on acid-free paper.

Library of Congress Cataloging-in-Publication Data has been requested.

ISBN: 978-1-4267-6637-4

18 19 20 21 22 23 24 25 26 27—10 9 8 7 6 5 4 3 2 1
MANUFACTURED IN THE UNITED STATES OF AMERICA

for James Rose Carroll and Mildred Lester Carroll
Parents of beloved memory who modeled "life in the Spirit"

Contents

Acknowledgments

The last few decades have offered a steady stream of books on the Holy Spirit, from a variety of perspectives, some of them conflicting and conflicted. This book does not attempt to settle such debates, nor does it set out to open up new interpretive vistas. Rather, my aim is more modest: (1) to provide a map for readers who have an interest in this intrinsically fascinating topic, (2) to help them gain a new appreciation of the variety of perspectives on the Spirit within the New Testament, and (3) to guide their further explorations through continuing study. My readers will discover signposts indicating some of the exciting work on the Spirit that scholars have been producing. The particular interest in this project, though, is a fresh encounter with the various treatments of the Holy Spirit, or Spirit of God, within the pages of the New Testament.

I am grateful to Warren Carter, chief editor of the Core Biblical Studies series of Abingdon Press and professor at Brite Divinity School, Texas Christian University, for the invitation to write this book. Warren's friendship and robust scholarship, his remarkable talents as an editor, and our shared commitment to ethically responsible biblical interpretation and to the value of wit and humor in serious scholarship make this collaboration especially meaningful to me. I express appreciation as well to the editorial and production staff at Abingdon Press for their skill in bringing this book to readers' hands and eyes.

As I have developed and honed the ideas that eventually made their way into this book, I have benefited greatly from the opportunity to present work-in-progress and receive instructive feedback from listeners in a number of settings. They are too numerous to mention here, but I single out the members of the Moveable Feast group of pastors and educators, who devoted a portion of their meeting in 2017 to a set of biblical texts addressing the Spirit; attendees at a Virginia Conference annual gathering of United Methodist alumni/ae of Union Presbyterian Seminary; and workshop participants at Union Presbyterian Seminary's "Seminary for a Day" and at a "Union on the Move" educational event cosponsored by the Coastal Carolina Presbytery. The privilege of learning alongside and from students in my classes at Union Presbyterian Seminary continues to invigorate me. For this project, the opportunity to supervise three students in directed studies on the Holy Spirit in the Bible—their initiative, not mine!—was especially formative, and I thank each of them: Carrie Cifers, Chad Beck, and Joshua Lewis. Joshua's intense commitment to deep and critical learning as a budding Pentecostal theologian offered important insight to me as a scholar who lacks direct experience of that tradition, for which awareness of the Spirit is so crucial.

Coinciding with my work on the Holy Spirit has been delightful collaboration with colleagues on the steering committee of the Society of Biblical Literature's Gospel of Luke Section. I am especially grateful for the friendship and collegial sharing I have enjoyed with my cochair Mark Matson, not least in drawing up plans for a session focused on the Spirit and the Gospel of Luke at the annual meeting of the society in November 2017. Fellow steering committee member Mikael Winninge has also been hard at work on a collaborative book-length study in Swedish. The time seems to be ripe for such undertakings! I also thank two eminent scholars from whose work on the Spirit I have learned immeasurably, Volker Rabens and Jack Levison. Their generous spirits have been very much in evidence in personal exchanges over the last couple of years. I am relieved that Volker's book on the New Testament and the Spirit will appear sometime after mine, as his erudition will no doubt put mine to shame. And as to Jack's publications on the Spirit, I am, well, deeply grateful for the inspiration I have drawn from his scholarship. (Pun intended, but the debt is immense, and no joke.)

I continue to enjoy teaching in the company of splendid faculty colleagues at Union Presbyterian Seminary. If one of the gifts of the Spirit to be discovered in the pages that follow is administrative skill, then my academic dean Ken McFayden is abundantly gifted. And if another of the gifts of the Spirit is eloquent preaching, then my president and Bible Department colleague Brian Blount—soon to serve a year's term as president of the Society of Biblical Literature—is likewise Spirit-gifted to an extraordinary degree. Just as important, I count them both as supportive colleagues and friends. I am truly grateful.

My mother, Mildred Lester Carroll, died in October 2016, two weeks shy of her ninety-seventh birthday. She knew I was working on this book, but this is my first publication that she did not have opportunity to learn about in our conversations. A friend of many years past, after receiving word of my mother's death, recently shared with me a recipe my mom gave her on the occasion of this childhood friend's wedding:

A Joyous Christian Life

Ingredients: Bible, devotional book, prayer, Holy Spirit

Read, study, meditate daily. Mix constantly with prayer. The most important ingredient is the Holy Spirit: Be filled with endless cups-ful. Share in faith, hope and—above all—love, with your husband, family, friends, and all with whom you come in contact.

Indeed. So you will gain a sense of why I dedicate this book to Mildred Lester Carroll and to my father, James Rose Carroll, both of blessed, Spirit-nourished memory.

Fresh from my first theological degree some thirty-five years ago, I had the good fortune of serving on the pastoral staff headed by Carl Gordon Howie, a distinguished scholar in his own right. Two of Carl's sermons are still vivid in my memory: "That's the Spirit!" and "God in the Ordinary." I learned from this wise scholar and preacher the importance of discerning the divine Spirit and the divine presence in people, moments, and places where one might not have expected to encounter it—not in the flashy, spectacular, and extraordinary, but in the ordinary. As I type these words early in January 2017, in the midst of particularly challenging "culture wars" in the United States and many other parts of the world, I am keenly aware of the importance of openness to the "new thing" that the divine presence, the Holy Spirit, may be fashioning in the midst of chaos and conflict and of the importance of active participation in that new thing by people of creativity and courage. So it is my hope that readers who are seeking to navigate these contemporary realities faithfully will find helpful pointers in the pages that follow, even when we are probing texts that are millennia old. The words of an ancient hymn are timely for a moment such as the present: *Veni Creator Spiritus* ("Come, Creator Spirit").

John T. Carroll
Richmond, Virginia
January 6, 2017

General Preface

This book, part of the Core Biblical Studies series, is designed as a starting point to New Testament study.

The volumes that constitute this series function as gateways. They provide entry points into the topics, methods, and contexts that are central to New Testament studies. They open up these areas for inquiry and understanding.

In addition, they are guidebooks for the resulting journey. Each book seeks to introduce its readers to key concepts and information that assist readers in the process of making meaning of New Testament texts. The series takes very seriously the importance of these New Testament texts, recognizing that they have played and continue to play a vital role in the life of faith communities and indeed in the larger society. Accordingly, the series recognizes that important writings need to be understood and wrestled with, and that the task of meaning making is complicated. These volumes seek to be worthy guides for these efforts.

The volumes also map pathways. Previous readers in various contexts and circumstances have created numerous pathways for engaging the New Testament texts. Pathways are methods or sets of questions or perspectives that highlight dimensions of the texts. Some methods focus on the worlds behind the texts, the contexts from which they emerge and especially the circumstances of the faith communities to which they were addressed. Other methods focus on the text itself and the world that the text constructs. And some methods are especially oriented to the locations and interests of readers, the circumstances and commitments that readers bring to the text in interacting with it. The books in this series cannot engage every dimension of the complex meaning-making task, but they can lead readers along some of these pathways. And they can point to newer pathways that encourage further explorations relevant to this cultural moment. This difficult and complex task of interpretation is always an unfolding path as readers in different contexts and with diverse concerns and questions interact with the New Testament texts.

A series that can be a gateway, provide a guide, and map pathways provides important resources for readers of the New Testament. This is what these volumes seek to accomplish.

Warren Carter
General Editor, New Testament
Core Biblical Studies

Abbreviations

General abbreviations

BCE . . . . before the common era

ca. . . . . *circa* = about, approximately

CE . . . . common era

cf. . . . . *confer* = compare

ch(s). . . . . chapter(s)

ed(s). . . . . editor(s), edited by, edition

e.g. . . . . *exempli gratia* = for example

esp. . . . . especially

ibid. . . . . *ibidem* = in the same place

i.e. . . . . *id est* = that is

mg. . . . . margin(al)

orig. . . . . original(ly)

repr. . . . . reprint(ed)

trans. . . . . translated by

v(v). . . . . verse(s)

vol(s). . . . . volume(s)

YHWH . . . . Hebrew (consonantal) letters signifying the divine name

Abbreviations of biblical books and other ancient writings

Gen . . . . Genesis

Exod . . . . Exodus

Lev . . . . Leviticus

Num . . . . Numbers

Deut . . . . Deuteronomy

1–2 Sam . . . . 1–2 Samuel

1–2 Kgs. . . . . 1–2 Kings

Neh. . . . . Nehemiah

Ps(s) . . . . Psalm(s)

Isa . . . . Isaiah

Jer . . . . Jeremiah

Ezek . . . . Ezekiel

Dan. . . . . Daniel

Mic . . . . Micah

Zech . . . . Zechariah

Matt . . . . Matthew

Rom . . . . Romans

1–2 Cor . . . . 1–2 Corinthians

Gal . . . . Galatians

Eph . . . . Ephesians

Phil . . . . Philippians

1–2 Thess . . . . 1–2 Thessalonians

Jas . . . . James

1 Pet . . . . 1 Peter

Heb. . . . . Hebrews

Rev . . . . Revelation

Wis . . . . Wisdom of Solomon

LXX . . . . Septuagint (Old Greek translation of the Old Testament)

Dead Sea Scrolls

1QH . . . . *Hodayot* = Thanksgiving Hymns (from Cave 1)

1QS . . . . *Rule of the Community* (from Cave 1)

Abbreviations of modern publications

AB. . . . . Anchor Bible and Yale Anchor Bible

AF. . . . . Apostolic Fathers

AGJU	Arbeiten zur Geschichte des antiken Judentums und des Urchristentums
ANF	Ante-Nicene Fathers
ANTC	Abingdon New Testament Commentary
BZNW	Beihefte zur Zeitschrift für die neutestamentliche Wissenschaft und die Kunde der älteren Kirche
CEB	Common English Bible
HTR	*Harvard Theological Review*
IBC	Interpretation Bible Commentary
IBT	Interpreting Biblical Texts
Int	*Interpretation: A Journal of Bible and Theology*
JETS	*Journal of the Evangelical Theological Society*
JPTSup	Journal of Pentecostal Theology Supplement Series
JSNTSup	Journal for Study of the New Testament Supplement Series
JSOTSup	Journal for Study of the Old Testament Supplement Series
LCL	Loeb Classical Library
LHBOTS	The Library of Hebrew Bible/Old Testament Studies
LNTS	Library of New Testament Studies
NovTSup	Supplements to Novum Testamentum
NRSV	New Revised Standard Version (of the Bible)
NTL	New Testament Library
NTT	New Testament Theology
SBLDS	Society of Biblical Literature Dissertation Series
SHBC	Smyth and Helwys Bible Commentary
SNTSMS	Society for New Testament Studies Monograph Series
SP	Sacra Pagina
WUNT	Wissenschaftliche Untersuchungen zum Neuen Testament
ZNW	*Zeitschrift für die neutestamentliche Wissenschaft und die Kunde der älteren Kirche*

Chapter 1

"That's the Spirit!": A Spirited Introduction to the Book

I begin this book about the Holy Spirit on a personal note. It was not until the final stages of my work on this project that I became aware of the degree to which it represents a resumption of unfinished business from two distinct periods of my life: my undergraduate days at the University of Tulsa in the 1970s and the start of my academic career as a young professor at Louisiana State University in the 1980s.

It was in students at Oral Roberts University across town, and in others influenced by that university and the holiness-charismatic ministry of its founder, that I first observed the enthusiasm of "Spirit ecstasy": speaking in tongues, fervent personal prayer, and the expectation that miracles can and do happen. This was all mystifying to me as a staid Presbyterian who was attending the "secular" (i.e., Presbyterian-affiliated) university in town.

A decade or so later, I found myself teaching in Baton Rouge, down the street from the thriving Pentecostal ministry of Jimmy Swaggart. Being a student of religion and equally curious about human psychology, I began to take notes on Swaggart's operation. I even developed a new course at Louisiana State University that focused on charismatic and Pentecostal movements. I was still trying to make sense of religious ideas and

1

practices that were foreign to me. And then things got *really* interesting. Jimmy Swaggart revealed to his congregation, and to the global audience listening in, that he had repeatedly succumbed to temptation and committed acts of sexual impropriety. Here was an obviously gifted musician and a charismatic, spellbinding preacher who had fallen in disgrace. How was I to make sense of all this? How could life "in the Spirit" be so disconnected from wise, ethical conduct? These formative experiences earlier in my life left me with any number of questions concerning what it means to talk about the Holy Spirit, or to claim the Spirit as legitimation for one's words and actions. Unfinished business—resumed in this book project.

The Holy Spirit, or Spirit of God, plays an important role in the writings of the New Testament and since their composition has been a major factor across nineteen centuries of Christian theological tradition. Yet the language and experiences associated with the Spirit have also bewildered many and have been the subject of diverse understandings. For example, it is common to think of the Spirit in terms of flashy, spectacular, extraordinary phenomena, such as ecstatic speech ("speaking in tongues"), prophecy, and miracles—phenomena viewed as matters of ecstatic experience, not intellectual activity or disciplined practice. Yet biblical texts also picture the Spirit as the source, guide, and inspiration for wisdom, skill, discernment, and ethical living. Other questions, too, have found a variety of answers: Is the Spirit an experience of all persons, or only of some? Is it an affair for individuals or (also) for communities? Is the evidence of the Spirit's activity to be seen primarily or even exclusively in postconversion, specially endowed capacities of the believer (spiritual *gifts*)? *Who* has the Spirit? What do we see when we say, "That's the Spirit!"? Important questions of religious identity and of group definition and belonging are in play in debates about the Holy Spirit. And so are important theological questions about the character and presence of God, and how humans experience the divine.

Indeed, intense debate about the Holy Spirit—in particular, the way in which the Spirit is related to God the Father and to the Son of God in a trinitarian theological understanding—lies at the root of a division in Christian churches that goes back at least to 1054 CE. The Roman

Catholic tradition, as it evolved in the Latin-speaking western part of the Mediterranean basin, came to affirm as a core belief that the Spirit, as a third member of the Trinity (God conceived as one, but also in three persons), "proceeds from the Father *and the Son.*" This was a sixth-century revision to the Nicene-Constantinopolitan Creed that had been adopted at a church-wide council of bishops in Constantinople in 381 CE, which tweaked the creedal formulation approved at Nicea in 325. The Greek-speaking churches in the eastern part of the Roman Empire rejected the phrase "and the Son" (*filioque* in Latin) as a deviation from the earlier agreement at Nicea. By the mid-eleventh century the Roman Catholic and Eastern Orthodox churches divided, in part over this disagreement about the Holy Spirit. This divide in Christianity continues to the present.

Filioque in the Nicene Creed: West vs. East

Roman Catholic	Eastern Orthodox
We believe in the Holy Spirit, the Lord, the giver of life, who proceeds from the Father and the Son, who with the Father and the Son is worshipped and glorified, who has spoken through the prophets.	And [I/we believe] in the Holy Spirit, the Lord, the creator of life, who proceeds from the Father, who together with the Father and the Son is worshipped and glorified, who spoke through the prophets.

The history of Christianity thus offers the Holy Spirit as an image of disunity, at least in part. The apostle Paul, however, pictures the Spirit as the source of unity for the believing community, though a unity that embraces diverse expressions and gifts (e.g., 1 Cor 12:4-11). Yet disagreement persists over just what the Spirit is and does, and how important a role it should play in the thinking and practice of faith communities.[1] Addressing an area of study that has been sometimes neglected and often debated, this book aims to offer readers fresh insight through careful attention to the various ways in which New Testament writings present and interpret the Spirit of God. Select bibliographies in each chapter will point the interested reader to an array of resources that can extend and deepen understanding through further study. First, though, it is well to ask what we are talking about when we invoke the language of *spirit*.

The Spirit and the Spirits: Language and Meanings

In both Hebrew (the language of nearly all the Tanak—the Old Testament or Hebrew Bible) and Greek (the language of the New Testament), the words typically translated *spirit* also carry the meanings of *breath* or *wind*: *rûaḥ* in Hebrew, and *pneuma* in Greek. Fascinating ambiguity in meaning results, for example, in the creation narrative in Genesis 1–2: the Spirit-wind of God moves as a creative energy over the waters of chaos (Gen 1:2), and God breathes the "spirit [*neshamah*] of life" into Adam (2:7). The imagery of spirit, wind, and life-bestowing breath converge. Similarly, in the Easter narrative of John's Gospel, Jesus breathes on the disciples and in so doing conveys the Holy Spirit (John 20:22). Earlier in this Gospel, the interplay of the connotations of wind and spirit allows Jesus to underscore the dynamic freedom of the Spirit, which is beyond human control (3:8).

Tanak: Jewish Scriptures

The label Tanak for the Jewish scriptures is an acronym that identifies its major sections:

Torah, the books of Moses

Nevi'im, the books of the (former and latter) prophets

Kethuvim, the writings, which include the Psalms and Wisdom books

---

Whether as wind, breath, or spirit, the *rûaḥ* or *pneuma* is not visible to the human eye, though its effects are evident, sometimes powerfully so (as in the Pentecost descent of the Spirit in Acts 2:1-13, for example). *Spirit* as an energizing, directing life-force is a quality of the human creature, and biblical texts therefore sometimes characterize the human self in terms of *spirit* (e.g., Luke 1:47; Acts 7:59; 1 Cor 4:21; Gal 6:18; Phil 4:23; 1 Thess 5:23). This human spirit is aligned with and ultimately derives from the divine Spirit, the unseen holy presence of God in the world and among human beings. "God is spirit," as John 4:24 puts it. However, spirit-beings can also be described as *unclean* or *evil* or demonic—unseen, malevolent beings from which human beings need to be liberated. Such unclean spirits often meet their match in the mission of Jesus, as narrated in the Gospels of Matthew, Mark, and Luke (the Synoptic Gospels), though no such dramatic encounters are told in the Gospel of John.

As Terence Paige has pointed out, the usual way of referring to these beings—intermediaries between the divine and human worlds—in the Greco-Roman world was not *pneuma* (spirit) but *daimōn* or *daimonion* (demon).[2] It was believed that they could be helpful or harmful to humans. But early Christian use of the term *spirits* for these beings, now viewed as harmful, malevolent forces opposing human flourishing, eventually influenced wider usage, as seen in Celsus's late-second-century CE critique of Christian beliefs (as reported in Origen, *Against Celsus*, 1.68) and in the Greek Magical Papyri from second- and third-century CE Egypt. Frequently in the New Testament Gospels, the terms *demon* and (*unclean*) *spirit* are used interchangeably. Luke 4:33-34, in which the categories of unclean spirit and demon are interchangeable, likely shows Luke's awareness that the customary Christian usage needs to be adapted for comprehension by other readers.

Early Christian notions about potent, unseen spiritual forces that contest the activity of Jesus and his followers are an important facet of the New Testament and of Christian beginnings. This would be a worthy topic for a book of its own. The focus in this book, however, will be on the Holy (divine) Spirit, not these adversarial *un*holy spirits.

Landmark Studies of the Spirit

With a book titled (in English translation) *The Influence of the Holy Spirit: The Popular View of the Apostolic Age and the Teaching of the Apostle Paul*, the eminent German biblical scholar Hermann Gunkel inaugurated a new era in the study of the Holy Spirit (the German work appeared in 1888). Gunkel emphasized the powerful, extraordinary effects of the Spirit and rooted early Christian views of the Spirit in Jewish religion. Both of these chords have been struck many times in the century and a quarter since. Recent decades have witnessed burgeoning interest in the topic, with substantial book-length treatments from a variety of perspectives. Among the important contributors to this research, many listed in the select bibliography at the end of the chapter, I would in particular point to Eduard Schweizer, James D. G. Dunn, Gordon Fee, Volker Rabens, Max Turner, Jürgen Moltmann, Michael Welker, Anthony Thiselton, Frank Macchia, and John R. (Jack) Levison. Space permits only a few brief summary notes—and a host of perceptive studies of portions of the New Testament must go unmentioned (though see the pointers to further reading in chs. 4–8 below).

- In an extensive article on the Spirit in the *Theological Dictionary of the New Testament* (English translation in 1968), in tandem with a book appearing in English under the title *The Holy Spirit* (1980), Schweizer highlighted the Spirit's role in generating prophetic proclamation.

- Dunn published two books in the 1970s in which he distinguished sacramental and Pentecostal views of "baptism in the Spirit" (1970) and probed the connection between Jesus and the experience of the Spirit (1975).

Baptism in the Spirit: Sacramental and Pentecostal Views

Sacramental View	Pentecostal View
Emphasizes Spirit-baptism as entry into the believing community, through participation in the sacrament of baptism	Emphasizes Spirit-baptism as dramatic event of empowerment for witness and service

- Fee, in a massive, magisterial exploration of the Spirit in the letters and theology of Paul (1994), offers the suggestive descriptor of "God's empowering presence" for the Holy Spirit. Fee contends that for Paul, the Spirit can actually make a real difference in the way people of faith live, so that they are no longer helpless captives to sin's domination.

- Rabens (2014), pushing back against arguments that Paul, under the influence of (e.g.) Stoic thought, viewed the Spirit as a material reality,[5] develops an interpretation of Paul's Spirit talk as metaphorical, relational, and relevant to ethics.

- Turner (2005, and earlier work on Luke-Acts) balances interest in the charismatic gifts of the Spirit (prophecy, ecstatic speech, etc.) and the Spirit's role in the salvation of God's people and their ethical commitment and practice.

- Moltmann, a prolific German systematic theologian, offers profound insight into the Holy Spirit. It is scarcely possible even to hint at the range and depth of Moltmann's thinking about the Spirit evident in several books and culminating in *The Spirit of Life: A Universal Affirmation* (1992).[6] Moltmann discusses the Spirit in a robustly trinitarian theological framework, and he develops that trinitarian sensibility out of narrative patterns (relating Father, Son, and Spirit) in the New Testament rather than on the basis of abstract metaphysics. Moltmann views the Holy Spirit as a power that fosters the life of the whole creation; he also highlights the subjective experience of the Spirit, but in social rather than individualistic terms. The Spirit "'destabilizes'...human systems of injustice" and "holds in life even self-destructive human communities in order to heal them."[7] The Spirit is to be found "in God's *immanence* in human experience, and in the *transcendence* of human beings in God."[8]

- Welker (1994), a creative German systematic theologian who also presents perceptive interpretations of biblical texts, accents the activity of the Spirit in fostering just human communities and prompting moves toward liberation.

7

- Thiselton, in a survey of views of the Holy Spirit in the Bible and in twenty centuries of theological tradition (2013, with a more compact treatment in 2016), engages critically yet sympathetically the work of evangelical and Pentecostal scholars, including the burgeoning scholarship on the Spirit in the Global South.

- Macchia (2006), a Pentecostal theologian who challenges many conventional notions among Pentecostal Christians as well as assumptions about their ideas and practices on the part of outsiders, urges that "baptism in the Spirit" be understood as more than a "high-voltage crisis experience" of postconversion charismatic gifting. Macchia places talk of the Spirit in a wider trinitarian and eschatological frame that connects both Spirit and Christ to the realization of God's reign in the "way of salvation."[9]

What Is Pentecostalism?
Pentecostal and Charismatic Views

Pentecostalism derives its name from the Feast of Pentecost, because Acts 2 records the first descent of the Spirit on believers at this festival, and Pentecostals regard themselves as heirs of that experience.

Pentecostal movements place emphasis on personal experience of the presence and power of the Spirit in Christian living.

Charismatic movements arise within established churches and traditions (including Catholic and Protestant churches) as renewal movements that, like Pentecostalism, emphasize experience of the Spirit as a lived reality.

For both Pentecostals and charismatics, personal encounter with the Holy Spirit is believed to empower individuals for witness and service, expressed in tangible gifts such as speaking in tongues and healing miracles.

- In a series of books (e.g., 2009, 2013) Levison challenges the assumption of a sharp distinction between the divine and human spirits and emphasizes the lifelong, Spirit-funded pursuit of wisdom and virtue, though not to the exclusion of ecstatic gifts of the Spirit.

The Approach of This Book

Before taking up New Testament perspectives on the Holy Spirit (in chs. 4–8), it is important to gain a sense of the various ways in which the identity and activity of the Spirit were presented in cultures and literature that informed the New Testament or its earliest audiences. So we begin in chapters 2 and 3 with surveys of the Spirit in the Jewish Bible (the Tanak) or (Christian) Old Testament, and in select writings from late Second Temple Judaism and from Greco-Roman authors outside Judaism.

Second Temple Judaism

The First Temple at Jerusalem was destroyed by Babylonian armies in 587–586 BCE. A successor temple was rebuilt ca. 515 BCE. This Second Temple, with major expansion begun by Herod the Great and continuing into the 60s CE, was destroyed by Roman armies in 70 CE. The last couple of centuries of this temple's existence are called late Second Temple Judaism. Much important Jewish literature comes from this period, including the book of Daniel, four books of the Maccabees (inspired by the crisis period of the Maccabean revolt, ca. 175 BCE), Wisdom literature, and an array of apocalyptic books such as 1 Enoch and writings from the Dead Sea Community (Dead Sea Scrolls).

Chapters 4–8 then discuss the distinctive views of the Holy Spirit in a set of New Testament books, primarily employing a literary close reading of the texts in which the Spirit figures. In chapter 4, the Gospels of Mark and Matthew claim attention, and in chapter 5 the two-volume work of Luke and Acts. Chapter 6 turns to the Gospel and First Letter of John, and chapter 7 features the letters of Paul. Finally, chapter 8 discusses the treatment of the Spirit in two of the General Epistles—1 Peter and

Hebrews—and then the book of Revelation. Chapter 9 rounds out the discussion of the Holy Spirit in the New Testament by observing a few of the trajectories of interpretation evident in the Christian theological tradition and exploring theological implications of the various New Testament takes on the Spirit.

For Further Reading

Burke, Trevor J. and Keith Warrington, eds. *A Biblical Theology of the Holy Spirit*. Eugene, OR: Cascade, 2014.

Dunn, James D. G. *Baptism in the Holy Spirit: A Re-examination of the New Testament Teaching on the Gift of the Spirit in Relation to Pentecostalism Today*. London: SCM, 1970.

———. *Jesus and the Spirit: A Study of the Religious and Charismatic Experience of Jesus and the First Christians as Reflected in the New Testament*. London: SCM, 1975.

Engberg-Pedersen, Troels. *Cosmology and Self in the Apostle Paul: The Material Spirit*. Oxford: Oxford University Press, 2010.

Fee, Gordon D. *God's Empowering Presence: The Holy Spirit in the Letters of Paul*. Peabody, MA: Hendrickson, 1994. Repr., Grand Rapids: Baker, 2011.

Gunkel, Hermann. *The Influence of the Holy Spirit: The Popular View of the Apostolic Age and the Teaching of the Apostle Paul*. Translated by R. A. Harrisville and P. A. Quanbeck II. Philadelphia: Fortress, 1979. Translation of *Die Wirkungen des heiligen Geistes nach der populären Anschauung apostolischen Zeit und der Lehre des Apostels Paulus*. Göttingen: Vandenhoeck and Ruprecht, 1888.

Kärkkäinen, Veli-Matti, ed. *Holy Spirit and Salvation: The Sources of Christian Theology*. Louisville: Westminster John Knox, 2010.

Levison, John R. *Filled with the Spirit*. Grand Rapids: Eerdmans, 2009.

———. *Inspired: The Holy Spirit and the Mind of Faith*. Grand Rapids: Eerdmans, 2013.

Macchia, Frank D. *Baptized in the Spirit: A Global Pentecostal Theology*. Grand Rapids: Zondervan, 2006.

Marshall. I. Howard, Volker Rabens, and Cornelis Bennema, eds. *The Spirit and Christ in the New Testament and Christian Theology: Essays in Honor of Max Turner*. Grand Rapids: Eerdmans, 2012.

Moltmann, Jürgen. *The Spirit of Life: A Universal Affirmation*. Translated by Margaret Kohl. Minneapolis: Fortress, 1992.

Paige, Terence. "Who Believes in 'Spirit'? *Pneuma* in Pagan Usage and Implications for Gentile Christian Mission." *HTR* 95 (2002): 417–36.

Prichard, Rebecca Button. *Sensing the Spirit: The Holy Spirit in Feminist Perspective*. St. Louis: Chalice, 1999.

Rabens, Volker. *The Holy Spirit and Ethics in Paul: Transformation and Empowering for Religious-Ethical Life*. 2nd ed. Minneapolis: Fortress, 2014. Orig. monograph WUNT 2/283. Tübingen: Mohr Siebeck, 2010.

Schweizer, Eduard. *The Holy Spirit*. Translated by Reginald H. Fuller and Ilse Fuller. Philadelphia: Fortress, 1980.

_____ "*Pneuma, Pneumatikos*." Pages 332–455 in vol. 6 of *Theological Dictionary of the New Testament*. Edited by Gerhard Kittel and Gerhard Friedrich. 12 vols. Grand Rapids: Eerdmans, 1968.

Thiselton, Anthony C. *The Holy Spirit—in Biblical Teaching, through the Centuries, and Today*. Grand Rapids: Eerdmans, 2013.

_____. *A Shorter Guide to the Holy Spirit: Bible, Doctrine, Experience*. Grand Rapids: Eerdmans, 2016.

Turner, Max B. *The Holy Spirit and Spiritual Gifts in the New Testament Church and Today*. Grand Rapids: Baker, 1997. Rev. ed. Peabody, MA: Hendrickson, 2005.

Welker, Michael. *God the Spirit*. Translated by John F. Hoffmeyer. Minneapolis: Fortress, 1994. Repr., Eugene, OR: Wipf and Stock, 2013.

Yong, Amos. *The Spirit Poured Out on All Flesh: Pentecostalism and the Possibility of Global Theology*. Grand Rapids: Baker, 2005.

Chapter 2

The Spirit in Jewish Scripture

One cannot begin a study of the Holy Spirit in the New Testament simply by reading the writings of the New Testament. The ways in which the Jewish scriptures (the Tanak or Christian Old Testament) present the language of *spirit* inform and shape early Christian talk about the Spirit of God. This chapter will explore a few significant strands in the Tanak.

Spirit or spirit in the Tanak?

To capitalize Spirit or not?

In discussing views of the s/Spirit (human and divine) in this chapter, I will use *Spirit* when the reference is to God (unless quoting from a translation that uses lower case) and *spirit* when the reference is to humans.

But there is significant interaction between the two spirit domains (divine and human) in the Tanak.

It is important to avoid reading later Christian theological (trinitarian) development of the Holy Spirit into these texts but instead to read them on their own terms.

The (Holy) Spirit of God in the Tanak

The word *rûaḥ*, signifying wind, breath, or spirit, appears some 380 times in the Tanak, with fifty-two of the occurrences falling within the book of Ezekiel alone. Most often, the Old Greek translation of the Hebrew Bible (LXX, or Septuagint) renders the Hebrew word *rûaḥ* as *pneuma*. *Pneuma*, too, can bear the meanings breath, moving air (wind), or spirit. The particular interest in this study is the *rûaḥ*, or *pneuma*, of God, although, as we will discover, the image of the divine *pneuma* as a creative, life-giving force resists an absolute distinction between the divine Spirit and the human spirit animated by it. The discussion to follow considers the Spirit as (1) the creative, life-giving power in the books of Genesis, Psalms, and Job; (2) the source of human wisdom and skill in the Pentateuch (the five books of Moses or Torah) and Daniel; (3) the source of extraordinary strength to effect deliverance in Judges; (4) the divine presence in the Psalms and Isaiah; (5) the restorative, life-giving power in Isaiah and Ezekiel; and (6) the eschatological gift of prophetic speech in Joel.

The Creative, Life-giving Spirit in Genesis, Psalms, and Job

The divine Spirit plays an important role in the Tanak beginning already in the account of creation in Genesis. God's wind-Spirit (*rûaḥ*) moves over the watery chaos, and the creation of the universe ensues (Gen 1:2). The human creature fashioned of earth then receives from the creator the life-breath (*neshamah*, 2:7), but this life-bestowing spirit-breath will have limited duration due to the pervasive moral corruption of human life (6:3). Genesis thus pictures God's Spirit-wind-breath as a cosmos-creating energy and also the source of human life as well as other forms of life (Gen 6:17; 7:15, 22).

Both the Psalms and the book of Job pick up this motif. As the righteous Job voices his protest against his undeserved suffering, he acknowledges that human creatures owe their very existence to the divine Spirit and that the continuation of life depends on the provision of life-breath from God (Job 27:2-4; 33:4; 34:14-15). This view of the creating, breath-supplying, life-bestowing role of the divine Spirit finds expression also in Israel's hymnbook of psalms (e.g., Ps 104:29-30). Not even the most powerful can escape the cessation of life and the return to earth-dust that attends the withdrawal of this life-force from God (Ps 146:3-4).

The Spirit as Source of Wisdom and Skill in the Pentateuch and Daniel

The Spirit of God, or spirit from God, not only creates and sustains life for earth-creatures who are otherwise mortal but also equips people with the wisdom and skill necessary to undertake important tasks. In this section, we will consider an array of Spirit-endowed characters in Genesis, the expansive narrative of the postexodus wilderness period (Exodus–Deuteronomy), and Daniel. In the next section, the Spirit's role empowering judge-deliverers in premonarchic Israel will claim attention.

After Joseph's ascent to power and influence in Egypt, supported by his well-deserved reputation as a discerning interpreter of dreams, the pharaoh receives favorably Joseph's systematic plan for food storage and distribution in preparation for a predicted famine. Egypt's ruler regards Joseph as one "in whom is the spirit of God" to an unsurpassed degree (Gen 41:38 mg.). The evidence for this claim? Joseph is the recipient of divine instruction, and thus possesses unparalleled discernment and wisdom (v. 39).

The book of Daniel offers a reprise of the spirit-wise Joseph in the character Daniel, who like Joseph must navigate the challenges of life in a foreign culture and court (now Babylonian), but who goes beyond his predecessor in his merging of remarkable wisdom and a life of unflinching fidelity to the norms and obligations of the Torah. In one of the entertaining court tales of Daniel 1–6, the Babylonian king Belshazzar is distressed when a mysterious hand inscribes a message on the wall of the royal palace (5:5-9). Not to worry, the queen assures him: "There is a man in your kingdom who has the spirit of holy gods in him!" (5:11 CEB mg.). This spirit is witnessed in his extraordinary wisdom and understanding (vv. 11-12). He can be summoned to interpret the message. The king repeats this vote of confidence in Daniel's spirit-enabled wisdom (v. 14), which the God-honoring Judean exile immediately puts on display. His inspired interpretation of a divinely sent message proves an unhappy one for the king, who meets swift demise as predicted by the visionary Daniel (vv. 24-30).

The narrative of the wilderness period after the exodus from Egypt also connects the divine Spirit to human wisdom and skill, first in the equipping of artisans for the fashioning of sacred vestments for the priest Aaron (Exod 28:2-3) and then for "a task of monumental proportions: to build a mobile tent in the wilderness to absorb God's presence" (see Exod 31:1-11; 35:30–36:6).[1] The artisan's skill in design and construction is credited to the wisdom that comes from the working of a spirit from God, resident within the human heart. His being filled with *rûaḥ* is equivalent to the giving of wisdom to the heart in 28:3; 31:3, 6; 35:31, 35. Bezalel and Oholiab are reported to have been Spirit-led not only to design and build but also to teach others to do so (35:34). Later, Joshua is said to be "a man who has the spirit," a worthy successor to Moses (Num 27:18). As Deuteronomy closes the book on Moses, that spirit-presence in Joshua is described as a fullness of "the spirit of wisdom," which had resulted from Moses's laying of hands on him (Deut 34:9 NRSV).

Moreover, seventy Spirit-endowed elders are appointed to assist Moses in tasks of leadership when the incessant complaints of a people inclined toward disobedience push him to his wit's end (Num 11:16-30). The seventy are equipped for their leadership role by being given a share in the s/Spirit that is present in Moses (11:17, 25). The Spirit has demonstrable effects, prompting prophetic speech (11:25, 27). Responding to Joshua's envious protest about the prophesying of Eldad and Medad outside the camp, Moses counters: "If only all the LORD's people were prophets with the LORD placing his spirit on them!" (v. 29; see also Joel 2:28-29!). This connection between Spirit inspiration and prophetic speech becomes increasingly important in later prophetic books. The precise sense of prophecy, left undefined in the Numbers text, remains for later elaboration, beginning already a few chapters later with the appearance of the prophet Balaam. Even as an outsider to the wandering Hebrew people, Balaam delivers a number of prophetic oracles, which, among other things, vigorously affirm God's blessing of this people—to the consternation of the Moabite leader Balak, who had commissioned Balaam's services as prophet (Num 22:1–24:25). Before the third oracle, an intriguing notice from the narrator indicates that Balaam did not in this instance use the prophetic technique of divination (seeking "omens," 24:1). Instead, "he turned toward the desert," and "God's spirit came on him" (vv. 1-2); the outcome is still more blessing for Israel. The Spirit as the source of prophetic inspiration will feature prominently in postexilic prophetic books and then in the New Testament.

The Spirit Empowers for Deliverance in the Book of Judges

Readers of the drama-filled book of Judges encounter repeated stories of Spirit-empowerment of a quite different kind. The narrative in Judges of the Hebrew people's experience after settling in Canaan is formulaic: again and again, religious disloyalty to YHWH[2] and moral corruption result in disaster, usually in the form of oppression by other peoples and interpreted as divine retribution. Then a Spirit-animated military deliverer arises to restore order and a measure of freedom. For example, of Othniel, the narrator comments, "The LORD's spirit was in Othniel, and he led Israel." That is, he "marched out for war" and brought military victory (Judg 3:10) and thus "the land was peaceful" (v. 11). Later, Gideon is "clothed" with Spirit power (6:34), on the way to an improbable, against-the-odds military triumph. The Spirit comes upon Jephthah, too (11:29), and the outcome is again victory in battle. Especially prominent is the Spirit's empowerment of Samson, endowing him with extraordinary strength (13:25; 14:6, 19; 15:14). The Spirit in Judges supplies empowerment for human agents of deliverance, but the Spirit's influence is temporary, just like the people's renewed loyalty to YHWH. It is striking, moreover, that these Spirit-inspired agents invariably exhibit disturbing character flaws themselves. In this succession of turbulent stories, equipping by the Spirit does not translate into moral virtue. This is an image of the Spirit's activity far removed from the heart-wisdom the Spirit's presence brings in passages mentioned in the previous section of the chapter.

17

We will turn next to the more serene and sublime image of Spirit as divine presence in the Psalms and Isaiah. First, though, a brief detour by way of the emergence of monarchic Israel—to observe the activity of spirits divine and otherwise in the story of Saul—provides a fitting segue from the turbulent saga of the Spirit in Judges. While Samuel is anointing Saul as the first king in Israel, he predicts that Saul will experience an ecstatic prophetic frenzy under the impulse of the divine Spirit (1 Sam 10:6), and the prediction is fulfilled immediately (vv. 9-12). The personal transformation by the presence of Spirit—gifting with another heart (v. 9)—is short-lived, however, and not permanent (v. 13; cf. 16:14). As Saul's story moves ahead to his eventual demise, *rûaḥ* re-enters in tragic mode. When the king proves less than fully obedient, the Spirit of the LORD abandons him, and Saul is then repeatedly tormented by an evil spirit said to have been sent by YHWH (1 Sam 16:14-23; 18:10; 19:9). Although Saul experiences relief from his agitation in spirit at the sound of David's music-making, the evil spirit's appearance puts David's life in jeopardy. So the activity of spirits divine and malevolent marks the beginning and ending of the monarchy of Israel's first king.

The Spirit as Divine Presence in the Psalms and Isaiah

In the passages discussed so far, *rûaḥ* is both a creative force or agency external to the human and a mode of divine influence (malevolent in the case of Saul) that has demonstrable effects within the character and capabilities of a person. Talk of the s/Spirit entails an interaction of divine and human spheres, with special interest in the gift of life itself and in the provision and intensification of human capacity, whether in the form of wisdom, skill, or strength. In both Israel's worship book (Psalms) and the latter portion of the book of Isaiah (a section termed Third Isaiah and dated to the postexilic period, perhaps fifth century BCE or later), the Spirit of God is a descriptor for the presence of God, especially as a life-giving, saving, restoring presence. Psalm 139 affirms that there is no place—not even Sheol, the domain for the dead—that the divine presence, referred to as God's Spirit, cannot reach (vv. 7-8).

Psalm 51 and Isaiah 63 exemplify the interplay of human and divine in language of the s/Spirit, and do so in contrasting ways. Psalm 51:10-12 pictures the working of the divine Spirit-presence in human life in positive, joyful terms: God's Spirit is the saving presence of God. The speaker of the psalm petitions God for a "new, faithful spirit" within: "Create a clean heart for me, God; put a new, faithful spirit deep inside me!" (v. 10). The next lines then cast the appeal in negative terms: "Please don't throw me out of your presence; please don't take your holy spirit away from me" (v. 11). The synonymous parallelism of "your presence" and "your holy spirit" signals clearly that for the psalmist God's holy spirit is an image of divine presence. Verse 12 completes the circle, returning to a positive appeal: "Return the joy of your salvation to me and sustain me with a willing spirit." The fruit of a persisting connection to divine, holy Spirit-presence is joyful assurance of salvation/deliverance and a human spirit attuned to the divine Spirit.

Holy Spirit = Divine Presence

Verbal parallels between Psalm 51 and Isaiah 63 show that the Holy Spirit can be an image for the holy, dynamic presence of God:

Psalm 51:11

Please don't throw me out of *your presence*;

please don't take *your holy spirit* away from me.

Isaiah 63:9-10 (NRSV)

It was no messenger or angel

but *his presence* that saved them. . . .

But they rebelled and grieved *his holy spirit*.

Isaiah 63:7-14 shows the other side of the coin. The speaker celebrates God's continuing acts of mercy and love for the benefit of Israel, even in moments of deep distress for the people: "It was no messenger or angel but [God's] presence that saved them" (v. 9 NRSV). Yet the people's history is one of repeated rebellion: "But they rebelled, and made God's holy spirit terribly sad, so that he turned into their enemy—he fought against them!" (v. 10). As in Psalm 51, the parallel drawn between God's saving presence and the Holy Spirit suggests that these are two ways of talking about the same thing—and not identical to heaven-dispatched angelic mediators. Despite the abundance of divine grace, the people spurned the holy Spirit-presence, and the result was more adversity. Their memory is persistent, though: "They remembered earlier times, when he rescued his people. Where was the one who drew them up from the sea? . . . Where was the one who put within them his holy spirit; the one who guided Moses' strong hand with his glorious arm; who split the water for them to create an enduring reputation for himself?" (Isa 63:11-12). Again here, the language of s/Spirit draws together the divine and human domains. The Holy Spirit is an external agency that acts for Israel's benefit, but it is also something that can be placed within the people. Isaiah 63 pictures the Holy Spirit as God's gracious, saving presence, yet a presence that can be resisted by a rebellious people. In the next section, we will discover that the prophet Ezekiel recognizes this dilemma and offers a profound resolution.

First, however, it is fitting to linger a bit longer in Third Isaiah to observe one other appearance of the Spirit. In a passage later taken up by Luke as a statement of Jesus's mission as prophet-Messiah (Luke 4:16-21), the speaker in Isaiah 61 declares: "The Lord God's spirit is upon me, because the Lord has anointed me. He has sent me to bring good news to the poor, to bind up the brokenhearted, to proclaim release for captives, and liberation for prisoners, to proclaim the year of the Lord's favor and a day of vindication for our God, to comfort all who mourn" (Isa 61:1-2).

Spirit-Anointed Prophets: Isaiah 61 and Luke 4

In Isaiah 61 (Third Isaiah, perhaps fifth century BCE), an anonymous Judean prophet announces a message of consolation promising liberation for an oppressed and suffering people.

Luke 4 has Jesus identify himself and his mission with the Spirit-anointed prophet who is the speaker of Isaiah 61:1-2.

The prophet continues with an array of images of divine grace for a formerly desolate, grieving Zion: "a crown in place of ashes," "oil of joy in place of mourning," "a mantle of praise in place of discouragement," "Oaks of Righteousness, planted by the LORD" (v. 3). The oracle engenders hope in future restoration of the nation's fortunes, even after "the devastations of many generations" (v. 4). So defeated and disconsolate human spirits will be revived by the bold message of a Spirit-inspired prophet.

The Restorative, Life-Giving Spirit in Ezekiel

The book of the prophet Ezekiel builds impressively on the notion that the *Spirit* is a way of talking about God's life-granting, saving, or restoring presence. Indeed, *rûaḥ* appears more than fifty times in Ezekiel, with the full range of the word's meanings (wind, breath, and s/Spirit). As wind, *rûaḥ* can be the instrument of divine judgment (e.g., Ezek 13:11, 13; 17:10; 19:12; 27:26). As breath, *rûaḥ* can give or restore life (e.g., 37:5-6, 8-10). And as s/Spirit, *rûaḥ* can set right human hearts and actions (e.g., 11:19; 36:26-27). As Robson has shown, the way Ezekiel associates divine word and spirit has to do less with "the inspiration and authentication of the prophet" than with the transformation—the moral renewal—of the people whom the prophet addresses.[3] In the language of s/Spirit in Ezekiel, we find once more an interplay of divine and human agency.

What Does Spirit Do in Ezekiel?

Positions Ezekiel for visionary experience

Prompts for a prophetic message

Brings about divine judgment (as wind)

Gives and restores life (as breath)

Sets humans right, creating the possibility for obedience and covenant-fidelity (as spirit): Ezekiel emphasizes that God provides the capacity for virtue displayed in human living.

But the book arrives at a vision of Spirit-engendered faithfulness in God's people only after grappling with the reality of persistent moral failure—deep reflection on the human predicament that rings true, given the context of national defeat and exile. Levison tracks the movement of the book toward greater and greater pessimism about human capacity for good. If virtue and obedience are to emerge, it will only be because God creates this capacity in the people. The Spirit is the instrument of this transformation.[4]

Ezekiel 18 imagines moral renewal that still lies within the reach of the prophet's audience. Verses 30-32 issue an appeal to turn away from persistent sin that merits ruin and to embrace instead the life that God purposes for the people. One of the images for this life of return and restoration is "a new and right spirit within" (v. 31). At this point in the book, the prophet directs listeners to obtain this right spirit: "*Make yourselves a new heart and a new spirit*" (v. 31).

Eighteen chapters later, however, the pathway to obedient hearts and actions must take account of the persistent inability of the people to "make themselves" what they need to be, to live faithfully and well. The picture now suggests sober realism about exile, death, and despair. Hope must spring from another source than the human heart and human capacity for good. How will a stubbornly disobedient and rebellious people find the ability to live in obedience and fidelity to God? In Ezekiel 36:22-28, God will give that capacity by placing Spirit-presence within the people. Thus they will be able to *live*: "I will give you a new heart and put a new spirit in you. I will remove your stony heart from your body and replace it with a living one, and I will give you my spirit so that you may walk according to my regulations and carefully observe my case laws" (vv. 26-27). What the people have repeatedly shown themselves unable to obtain for themselves God will provide: a new heart, a heart of flesh, a new spirit.

The reality of defeat and exile—indeed, the painful history of a nation divided, reaching back some five centuries to the post-Solomon era—calls not only for personal restoration (Ezek 36) but also for national restoration. Ezekiel imagines God doing something on the latter, larger scale too. In chapter 37, the Spirit is again the source of restoration and of renewed life. With bold images, the prophet pictures a future in which God will do for Israel what the people cannot do, nor can they scarcely imagine: a people and national unity restored as if life were being breathed back into scattered, dry bones.

In Ezekiel 37:1-14, cascading images of death, life, and renewal picture God restoring spirit-breath, and hence life and hope, to a dispirited, divided, and exiled people. God's Spirit moves Ezekiel to this remarkable visionary experience: "The LORD's power overcame me, and while I was in the LORD's spirit, he led me out and set me down in the middle of a certain valley. It was full of bones" (v. 1; cf. 2:2; 3:12-14, 24; 11:1, 24). The ensuing dialogue between prophet and YHWH (or YHWH's Spirit) establishes that life can be restored to these dry bones but only by God— and only by the divine Spirit-breath. The prophet is instructed to deliver the message "The LORD God proclaims to these bones: 'I am about to put breath [*rûaḥ*] in you, and you will live again'" (37:5). After Ezekiel speaks the message as directed, bones, flesh, and skin reassemble, but the bodies remain lifeless, without breath (vv. 7-8). So the prophet is instructed to summon the breath (*rûaḥ*) "from the four winds" and to "breathe into these dead bodies and let them live" (v. 9). The result is that "an extraordinarily large company" lives again (v. 10).

Ezekiel's vision then receives its interpretation: the lifeless bones are "the entire house of Israel," whose hope has been extinguished (v. 11). God will restore the people to the land, as if calling the dead back to life (v. 12). And picking up the thread from 36:22-28, the passage concludes with the image of the divine Spirit placed within the people: "I will put my spirit in you, and you will live" (37:14 mg.). Not only moral renewal but also the gift of (restored) life itself come only from God. The Spirit is the agent and life-breath is the vivid, vivifying image of God's action. Thus the prophet seeks to engender hope in a defeated, despairing people in the context of exile.

The Eschatological Spirit as Gifting for Prophecy in Joel

The Spirit does far more in the Tanak than simply—though impressively—inspire prophetic speech. However, this dimension of the Spirit's activity, which looms so large in New Testament appropriations of Jewish Spirit traditions, does figure prominently in the Jewish scriptures. We have already seen glimpses of this activity of the Spirit in the narrative in Numbers (11:25, 27, 29; 24:1-2), and the divine Spirit is also associated with the activity of prophets in Isaiah 61:1 and Ezekiel (e.g., 11:5, 24; 37:1). The books of the earlier prophets (e.g., Amos, Isaiah, and Jeremiah) generally do not establish the credentials and authenticity of the prophet and his message by invoking Spirit-inspiration. Perhaps contested claims to inspiration led to some reticence. Whatever the reasons, later texts—beginning with Ezekiel, as we have already discovered—do link prophetic speech to the Spirit. Zechariah 7:12 and Nehemiah 9:30 both offer retrospective commentary on the activity of Israel's earlier prophets, claiming both that they were Spirit-inspired and Spirit-tutored and that the people invariably resisted their teaching.

An especially bold linking of the Spirit and prophecy appears in Joel 2:28-32 (3:1-5 LXX), another passage that Luke will employ to illumine the story he is telling (Acts 2:17-21; cf. Isa 61:1-2, cited in Luke 4:18-19). Like Psalm 51 and Isaiah 63, Joel associates the Spirit with divine presence. Even now, God is present among the people: "You will know that I am in the midst of Israel, and that I am the LORD your God—no other exists" (Joel 2:27). In the future that Joel imagines, this presence will become a Spirit lavishly "poured out" on the people to foster a capacity for prophetic discernment and speech (v. 28). The most astonishing claim here is the wide scope of the divine gifting for prophecy, which the prophet declares will come to the whole people—young and old, male and female, across boundaries of social and household status: "After that I will pour out my spirit upon everyone; your sons and your daughters will prophesy, your old men will dream dreams, and your young men will see visions. In those days, I will also pour out my spirit on the male and female slaves" (vv. 28-29). The Spirit flows from God, lavishly coming upon any and all, funding the imaginative vision that forms and informs prophetic speech. Prophets of the future age will be equipped by God to speak on behalf of God ("Thus says the LORD") to the people. Once again, divine agency and initiative collaborate with human agency, here in prophetic mode.

For another of the minor prophets, Micah, not all prophetic speech is legitimate; some prophets do not actually speak for God. Prophets who tailor their message according to the payment received (or not) will find themselves in the dark, without vision, without revelation—without a word from God to declare, and thus disgraced (Mic 3:5-7). Micah himself, by contrast, is "filled with power, with the spirit of the LORD" (3:8a). To what effect? The Spirit empowers a commitment to justice and to truth-telling that confronts Israel with its sin (v. 8b). Here and elsewhere in the Tanak, as well as the New Testament, a prophet's message attuned to the divine commitment to justice and truth is stamped by the Spirit, and as such can claim attentive hearing.

And How Does All This Matter for the New Testament?

As we have seen at a number of points in the above sketch, New Testament writings draw much imagery and description for the Holy Spirit from Tanak (Old Testament) texts. It may be helpful in closing the chapter to give a few examples of the thematic continuity between the Testaments in their depictions of the divine Spirit, even if the connections usually do not take the form of quoted phrasing. (Luke 4:18-19 and Acts 2:17-21 are remarkable exceptions, with their quotations of Isa 61:1-2 and Joel 2:28-32, respectively.)

• In both Isaiah 63:7-14 and the Psalms (51:10-12; 139:7-12), the language of the Spirit points to the holy presence of God in Israel's experience. In the New Testament, Paul draws assurance from the experience of the Spirit—of God as a saving presence— even in the depths of human suffering (Rom 5:3-5; 8:26-39).

• Often, passages in the Tanak ascribe an array of human abilities to the influence of the divine Spirit: wisdom (Gen 41:38-39; Dan 5:11-12, 14), leadership (Num 11:16-30), skill in craft (Exod 28:2-3; 31:1-11; 35:30–36:6), and prophetic speech (Joel 2:28-32; Zech 7:12; Neh 9:30; Ezekiel). In the New Testament, Paul emphasizes the Holy Spirit's provision of various gifts for leadership and service, including wisdom and prophetic speech (1 Cor 12:4-11, 28). John's Gospel, too, attributes human wisdom (especially the ability to discern and speak the truth) to the activity of the divine Spirit (John 14:26; 16:13-15). Luke and Acts highlight courageous prophetic witness, again animated by the Holy Spirit (e.g., Luke 1:68-79; 2:27-35; 4:16-21; Acts 2). Moreover, Paul insists that the trademark product of the Spirit's activity in the community of believers is love (e.g., 1 Cor 12–13; Gal 5), and in Romans the Holy Spirit is the engine for the moral life (Rom 8:1-17). This conviction draws from Ezekiel's picture of the covenant people's fidelity and obedience empowered by God's Spirit placed within them (Ezek 36:22-28; 37:1-14).

- In Genesis 1–2, and also in Job and the Psalms, the Spirit creates and sustains life (Gen 1:2; 2:7; Job 27:2-4; 33:4; 34:14-15; Ps 146:3-4). When breath-spirit ceases, death results. Yet Ezekiel offers God's Spirit-wind-breath as a power that restores life (Ezek 36:22-28; 37:1-14). In the New Testament, too, the Spirit of God generates life (Matt 1:18, 20; Luke 1:35), and death follows when life-breath (spirit) leaves (Matt 27:50; John 19:30). But for Jesus (Rom 1:4; 8:11) and God's people alike, the divine Spirit gives resurrection life (Rom 1:4; 8:11; 1 Cor 15:42-57). So the presence and activity of the Holy Spirit, both in prophetic speech and in death-defeating life-energy, draws the future reality into the present experience of the people of God as an eschatological (end-time) phenomenon (Joel 2:28-32; Ezek 37:1-14; Acts 2:17-21; Rom 8; 1 Cor 15).

The discussion of New Testament presentations of the Holy Spirit in chapters 4–8 will explore these thematic possibilities more fully. First, though, a brief tour in chapter 3 of Jewish and Greco-Roman literature closer in time to the New Testament writings will offer further helpful orientation.

For Further Reading

Block, Daniel I. "The Prophet of the Spirit: The Use of *RWH* in the Book of Ezekiel." *JETS* 32 (1989): 27–49.

Hildebrandt, Wilf. *An Old Testament Theology of the Spirit of God*. Peabody, MA: Hendrickson, 1995.

Levison, John R. *Filled with the Spirit*. Grand Rapids: Eerdmans, 2009.

———. *Inspired: The Holy Spirit and the Mind of Faith*. Grand Rapids: Eerdmans, 2013.

———. *The Spirit in First Century Judaism*. AGJU 29. Leiden: Brill, 1997.

Ma, Wonsuk. *Until the Spirit Comes: The Spirit of God in the Book of Isaiah*. JSOTSup 271. Sheffield: Sheffield Academic, 1999.

Montague, George T. *The Holy Spirit: Growth of a Biblical Tradition*. New York: Paulist, 1976.

Robson, James Edward. *Word and Spirit in Ezekiel*. LHBOTS 447. London: T and T Clark, 2006.

Schuele, Andreas. "The Spirit of YHWH and the Aura of Divine Presence." *Int* 66 (2012): 16–28.

Chapter 3

The Spirit in Second Temple Literature and Greco-Roman Culture

As first-century people inhabiting the Greco-Roman world, New Testament authors and readers thought and spoke about the s/Spirit under the influence of other notions current in their cultural environment. Certainly, what they had to say about the Spirit of God was *heard* in relation to such ideas. This chapter will consider a few early Jewish and Greco-Roman sources of particular interest for readers of the New Testament, including the Dead Sea Scrolls and writers such as Philo and Josephus. Because the survey covers many centuries and cultures, and a diverse array of writings, the treatment must be selective and compact.

Holy Spirit in Early Jewish Writings

A popular modern view maintained that in the period after the prophets the Spirit was thought to have vanished from Israel. However, many Jewish writings from the late Second Temple period do attest continuing reflection on the Spirit and its influence on human capabilities.[1] Here we will attend to just a few of these sources: the Dead Sea Scrolls, the Wisdom of Solomon, the prolific Alexandrian statesman and philosopher Philo, and the historian Flavius Josephus.

The Dead Sea Scrolls

Among the many manuscripts discovered in the caves near the Qumran settlement at the Dead Sea (second century BCE–first century CE), some offer an interesting glimpse of this community's view of the divine Spirit and its relation to the human spirit. The word *rûaḥ* appears more than two hundred times in the extant scrolls, and of these about three dozen refer to a divine Spirit. Other passages point to the human spirit, angelic or demonic beings, and wind or breath.

In the *Rule of the Community*, one encounters a view of the world and of human life as dominated by a contest between two spirits, one good and the other evil (1QS III, 13–IV, 26). These spirits are variously described as spirits of truth versus deceit, of justice versus injustice— with human speech and actions corresponding to the influencing power. These spirits are thus both forces outside the person and subjective impulses within, whether for good (truth and fidelity) or evil (falsehood and disobedience). In this polarity of opposing spirits, persons are predisposed from birth onward to a life shaped by one or the other (1QH XV, 6-32). Ultimately, God will restore community members by a purifying "spirit of holiness" or "spirit of truth" (1QS IV, 20-22). Elsewhere in the Scrolls, the accent falls on the Spirit's activity as an eschatological (end-time) phenomenon and as the "basis and source of [the community's] spirituality."[2]

In the Thanksgiving Hymns scroll (1QH), it is through the agency of the Holy Spirit that the speaker/singer is gifted with knowledge of God and of divine mysteries. The Spirit is the source of revelation (1QH XX, 11-12) and thus of the instruction community members receive to live a life of fidelity to God. This is an uphill battle, though; the hymns paint a stark picture of human failure, with the potent influence of a "spirit of error and depravity" as one of the reasons (IX, 21-23). The divine Spirit intervenes, however, to purify, to restore the human capacity to know and practice truth—though only for members of the sectarian group, not for outsiders.

Wisdom of Solomon

The wisdom book associated—in a fictional device—with the classic exemplar of royal wisdom, King Solomon, probably comes from a Hellenistic Jewish author in first-century BCE Alexandria (Egypt). The book, which is included in the Old Testament Apocrypha, refracts Jewish biblical teaching through the prism of Stoic and Middle Platonist ideas (see below). In the Wisdom of Solomon, *pneuma* appears as a life-infusing, virtue-engendering, justice-fostering principle in humans, received from God for the duration of one's existence (Wis 1:3-8; 2:2-3; 7:22–8:11; 15:11, 16; 16:14). The spirit is "identified with the gift of wisdom," and it directs a life of discipline and wise, holy conduct.[3] If "God doesn't love anything as much as people who make their home with Wisdom" (7:28), it is the divine Spirit that guides and animates such a life of wisdom.

This is not an affair for individuals in isolation, however: the divine s/Spirit also fills the whole universe, fashioning and renewing all things (1:7; 7:22, 24, 27; 8:1; 12:1). God's "imperishable spirit is present in all things" (12:1) and after the pattern of Stoic thought orders and gives coherence to the cosmos (1:7). In a lengthy catalog of the qualities that mark the "spirit of wisdom" (7:22–8:1), readers meet in the divine Spirit not only evidence of God's holy transcendence but also God's active presence and engagement in the world.[4] The accent in the Wisdom of Solomon on the agency of the Spirit does not evacuate humans of moral agency, for they must turn away from the deceit, error, and injustice that are incompatible with the character of the divinely given "spirit of wisdom": "Wisdom will avoid a deceptive soul that plans evil. Wisdom won't make her home in a body that is devoted to sin. A holy, instructive spirit will flee deceit and leave when ignorant people start to plot. It is ashamed to be found in the presence of wrongdoing" (1:4-5). The holy spirit within a person is capable of receiving instruction in wisdom but must remain committed to that life-path. The virtue cultivated by the spirit of wisdom is not something automatic but entails holy discipline.[5]

Stoicism and Middle Platonism

Both the Wisdom of Solomon and the writings of Philo of Alexandria show considerable influence from two intellectual-philosophical traditions that were especially important in the period of late Second Temple Judaism and of Christian origins. Below you will find listed a few trademark features of these approaches to thought and life.

Stoicism

Key figures include Zeno (founder in early third century BCE), Cleanthes, Chrysippus, and in the first century CE Seneca.

Divine principle of rationality (logos) gives coherence, meaning, and purposefulness to the world.

The good in human life follows from living in accordance with reason, and thus in harmony with nature, accepting what is.

A life of self-sufficiency is possible across lines of status and position.

Middle Platonism

Origins in the Academy of Plato, a student of Socrates at Athens (fourth century BCE)

Basic to the Platonist worldview is a distinction between (1) the world of sensation and ordinary experience and (2) the true reality consisting of ideas or forms.

In Middle Platonism, Plato's philosophy was calibrated under the influence of other views such as Stoic ethics and the philosophy of Aristotle.

Key figures include Philo, Plutarch, and Apuleius.

It emphasizes the transcendence of the Supreme Mind, or God, who can be reached only through a chain (hierarchy) of being—only indirect knowledge of this Supreme Mind is possible.

Thus Middle Platonist views of the human and of the cosmos are dualistic, distinguishing the sensible-physical domain from that of intellect or spirit.

Middle Platonism mediated the Platonist intellectual heritage to the third-century CE revival of Platonism in Plotinus and Porphyry.

Philo

A sophisticated Jewish intellectual writing in Alexandria (Egypt) in the first half of the first century CE, Philo presented allegorical expositions of biblical texts such as the Genesis creation accounts. Under the influence of both Stoic ideas and Platonist thought, he interpreted Jewish sacred texts out of and for Hellenistic culture. In his voluminous writings, Philo employs *pneuma* in various ways: as the divine Spirit with reference to the deity or in relation to humankind or the cosmos, and as the prophetic spirit.[6] Only a brief sketch is possible here.

Philo returned again and again to Genesis 2:7, with its image of the divine in-breathing into the human creature. Though much influenced by the Stoic notion of *pneuma* as a fiery aether that pervades the cosmos as a unifying power (e.g., Philo, *On the Creation of the World* 131), Philo pushes back against the physics of a material *pneuma*. Instead, an immaterial divine creator as "immortal spirit descends as the mind to inhabit a mortal body" (ibid., 134–135).[7] It is the purest form of the soul (*psychē*)—rationality of mind—that represents human contact with the divine. Indeed, the creation of the human in the divine image and the breathing-in of soul means "a full infusion of deity."[8] And with that participation in deity comes the capacity also for virtue and for intimate knowledge of God (e.g., Philo, *Allegorical Interpretation of Genesis* 1.33–38). In a fascinating reading of Genesis 2, Philo distinguishes between breath and spirit; only the latter (*pneuma*) possesses vigor and power, and God breathes this potency only into the higher part of the soul, the reasoning mind (ibid., 1.39–42).

Despite the endowment with spirit-strength evident in the capacity for reason, Philo pictures a counterpoint to this divine Spirit in the tug "downward" to passion and bodily necessity (ibid., 2.27–30). So, it turns out, there are two categories of persons, "those who live by reason, the divine inbreathing,... [and] those who live by blood and the pleasure of the flesh"; the latter are composed of a "clod of earth," the former are "the faithful impress of the divine image" (*Who Is the Heir of Divine Things?* 57).[9]

Philo's reflection on the figure of Moses develops the role of the divine Spirit also in prophetic inspiration (e.g., *Life of Moses* 2.264–265; *On the Decalogue* 175). Other individuals, too, are inspired by the divine Spirit to understand and interpret the truth, for example, Abraham (*On the Virtues* 217) and Balaam (*Life of Moses* 1.277). How does this prophetic inspiration happen? A prophet is an interpreter "prompted by Another in all his utterances"; human thought cedes place to "a new visitor and tenant, the Divine Spirit," which dictates the prophetic message (*On the Special Laws* 4.49). This is a temporary, exceptional supplanting of human reason by the prophecy-inducing divine Spirit (*Who Is the Heir of Divine Things?* 259).[10] Philo's view of prophetic oracles as the product of temporary possession not directed by human intellect resembles the understanding of inspiration assumed for the oracle at Delphi (see below)—a notion that may be traced to Plato, though not using the word *pneuma* (e.g., *Meno* 99C–D; *Phaedrus* 244A–245C, 265B; *Ion* 533D–534E). Philo can cast his own skill as an interpreter of Jewish scriptures as the result of this same extraordinary operation of the divine Spirit, though clearly not disconnected from his own intellectual activity and acuity (*On Dreams* 2.252; *On the Migration of Abraham* 34–35).[11]

Josephus

The first-century Jewish historian Flavius Josephus, a native of Jerusalem who later resided for some three decades in Rome, wrote extensive accounts of the Jewish War against Rome (66–74 CE) and of the entire history of the Jewish people (*Jewish Antiquities*), as well as a treatise in defense of the Jewish religion and people (*Against Apion*). Coursing through his writings is a strong interest to offer a favorable picture of the Jewish people and religion. In his elaborate retelling of biblical narratives, Josephus often omits references to the Spirit.[12] But not always. Second Chronicles 7:1 reports that "fire came down from heaven," and filled the temple. This image suggests to Josephus the divine Spirit, composed (as in Stoic thought) of fire and air (*Jewish Antiquities* 8.118). And Josephus regularly links the Spirit to prophetic activity (ibid., 4.118; 6.166, 222–23; 8.408). In a fashion reminiscent of Philo, Josephus credits the prophetic insight of Balaam (Numbers 22–24) to the activity of an intrusive spirit, not the seer's own intellectual acuity (*Jewish Antiquities* 4.118–121).[13] Josephus also associates the divine Spirit with the wisdom of Daniel, adapting the biblical account to make explicit that the source of Daniel's wisdom is not *a* spirit interior to him but *the* Spirit—an external agent that accompanies him (ibid., 10.239).[14] The Jewish historian and apologist develops imagery of divine presence, including the Spirit, in a way that accords with sensibilities and assumptions of his Roman literary audience.

Spirit in Other Greco-Roman Authors

As Terence Paige has shown, there is no clear evidence, prior to or during the course of the first century CE, of the use of the word *pneuma* to refer to spiritual beings (whether good or malevolent) in Hellenistic sources apart from early Judaism or Christianity. Instead, intermediaries between the divine and human worlds are called *daimones* or *daimonia* (demons). It is possible that interaction with early Jewish and Christian use of *pneuma* for spirit-beings contributed to the adoption of this language in sources such as the Greek Magical Papyri and Celsus (late second century CE, as reported in Origen, *Against Celsus* 1.68). Further, divine inspiration of poets and prophets (oracles) was generally not pictured as due to the operation of a *pneuma*. Claims for the presence and potency of *pneuma* (spirit) beyond early Jewish and Christian circles should be more cautious than many scholars have suggested.[15] Nevertheless, extant literature does offer some insight worth our attention. According to Hesiod (ca. 700 BCE), the Muses (daughters of Zeus) breathe into (*empneō*) the poet "a divine voice" and he is then able—and tasked—to "glorify what will be and what was before," and to "sing of the race of the blessed [gods], who always are" (*Theogony* 29–33). Plato's Socrates attributes to divine inspiration the composition of the poet and the prophetic speech of the oracle, though without using the word *pneuma* for this divine influence (*Phaedrus* 244A–245C; *Ion* 533D–534E). Within the space available here, however, the focus will be on Stoic ideas about the *pneuma*, the prophetic Oracle of Delphi, and the notion of the *numen* or divine spirit of the emperor and the imperial family.

Stoics: Pneuma as Unifying Element in the Cosmos

Stoic physics developed a view of the cosmos as ruled by a divine mind (*nous*) and permeated by *pneuma*, an aether composed of fire and air. The Stoic philosopher Seneca, writing mid-first century CE, includes in a sketch of Stoic ideas the affirmation that "a single divine and all-pervading spirit" unifies the whole cosmos (*On the Nature of the Gods* 2.19).[16] Similar views are credited to the third-century BCE teacher Chrysippus and (by Diogenes Laertius in *Lives of the Philosophers* 7.139) to another Stoic teacher, Antipater of Tyre.[17]

Diogenes Laertius's summary of Stoic beliefs includes the notion that the cosmos is a living being, endowed with rationality and soul—a mixture of fire and air that composes *pneuma* and holds the cosmos together (ibid., 7.142).[18] In Stoic cosmology, this *pneuma* was matter, a substance, as seen, for example, in a mid-third-century CE apologetic treatise by the Christian writer Origen. Origen ascribes to the Stoics the notion that God is Spirit (*pneuma*), "interpenetrating everything and containing everything" within itself (Origen, *Against Celsus* 6.71.4–12).[19] Celsus claims that Christians share this notion of God as *pneuma*, hence as material (embodied) and perishable, assertions that Origen counters (ibid., 6.70–71).

For the Stoics, spirit was not just impersonal matter effecting cosmic coherence but also a factor in the human self. Among third-century BCE medical writers in Alexandria (Egypt), perception and movement could be regarded as the effect of *pneuma*.[20] In one of his letters, Seneca (first century CE) links the cosmos-unifying spirit to a "holy spirit [that] indwells within us" (*sacer intra nos spiritus*), which descends in order to give humans a "knowledge of divinity," though it still "cleaves to its [heavenly] origin"—the human soul as a fragment of the cosmic soul ("On the God within Us," *Moral Epistles* 41.2, 5). A person tutored by the holy spirit dwelling within lives in accord with reason, which is to say in harmony with one's own nature.[21]

The Oracle at Delphi: Spirit of Prophecy?

Especially noteworthy among temples featuring inspired oracles was the Pythia, or Oracle of Delphi, the oracle-pronouncing priestess at the temple of Apollo in Delphi (across the Gulf of Corinth from the city of Corinth). Plutarch (ca. 45–125 CE), a prolific Middle Platonist writer who served for a time as priest at the temple, later wrote about the prophetic oracle, the "mantic *pneuma*" ("On the Decline of Oracles," in the essay collection *Moralia*). He explains the oracle's inspiration as the result of a vapor that enters the prophetess from a chasm below the temple building, a view similar to that articulated by the Stoic philosopher Cicero in the mid-first century BCE (*On Divinations* 1.79). This appears to have been a local tradition at Delphi, not a widespread view that prophetic inspiration at various oracular sites was produced by a holy vapor (*pneuma*). The ingesting of water, blood, or plant leaves would be the precursor to prophetic speech in other shrines.[22] Whether the inspiration derived from spirit-vapor as in Delphi or from other materials of earth, people of the Greco-Roman world understood that the gods could communicate via prophetic oracles.

The Numen of the Roman Emperor and the Spirit of the Divine Family

In Roman society, the cohesion of the family was fostered, among other things, by religious devotion within the household, and one focus of worship was the *genius*, an unseen spiritual life-force in which all family members shared—especially the head of the household, the *paterfamilias*.

This spiritual potency guarded family members while they were alive and ensured the continuation of the family line into the future.[23] Related to the *genius* was the *numen*, the expression of the will of a divine being. The supreme *paterfamilias* was the emperor. So it is unsurprising that as expressions of religious devotion to the current emperor and to the imperial family (the imperial cult) grew in importance in the first century CE, the *genius* and *numen* of the emperor were among the spiritual forces to be reckoned with.

Jews and Christ believers alike would have difficulty incorporating into their social-religious practice devotion to the emperor's *numen* or *genius*, the spirit-manifestations of his divinity. For followers of Christ, the Holy Spirit of the sovereign God and of the *kyrios* (Lord) Jesus was not simply one of these spiritual forces mediating between the human and divine worlds. The Holy Spirit, for them, was *the* divine life-force interacting with the human world. Some Christians in the second and third centuries CE would refuse to express reverence for the divine spirit of the imperial family or for the *genius* of the emperor, even at the cost of their lives.[24]

Conclusion: Summary and Pathways to the New Testament

The writings and perspectives touched on in chapters 2 and 3 span many centuries, religious traditions, and cultures. So it is scarcely possible to draw the findings of this selective survey into a neat synthesis. Certainly, we have encountered a wide range of understandings of the divine, human, and cosmic spirits. At many points, a dynamic interaction between the divine (or cosmic) and human spirits has surfaced, and within that dynamic a coinciding of divine and human agency. In both early Jewish and other Greco-Roman arenas, one important strand concerning the Spirit has to do with the divine inspiration of prophetic discourse—often as an aid, not a replacement, to human intellectual striving. This impact of the Spirit on prophetic vision and speech in the human community figures prominently in the New Testament as well. Across many writings and genres within the Tanak, however, the *rûaḥ* or *pneuma* assumes a variety of other distinct roles. The Spirit is a creative, life-giving force; the source of human wisdom and skill; the agent of deliverance from enemy domination; a way of representing divine presence; and a force for restoration of both life and moral capacity. Many of these facets of the Spirit's character and activity will have an important influence on New Testament texts. When we turn to developments of the imagery of s/Spirit in the New Testament, we will need to attend closely to the specific ways in which the Holy Spirit is presented in each writing. Especially given the prominence in Stoic thought of a world-pervading, reason-fostering (aether) spirit, early Greco-Roman audiences may be keenly interested in points of convergence and divergence between the message of Christ followers and Stoic ideas. In the letters and thought of Paul, in particular, his use of the language of body and spirit to shape the moral practice of his faith communities has resonance with Stoic ideas.

Even the selective tour of "Spirit sites" in the cultural world of the New Testament in chapters 2 and 3 makes clear that the earliest Christ believers—both the New Testament authors and the audiences for which they wrote—were not the first or only ones to talk about or have experience of the divine Spirit, the Holy Spirit. In Jewish literature and tradition, the Spirit was more than just a spirit inspiring prophecy, and a variety of documents from late Second Temple Judaism (including the Wisdom of Solomon, the Dead Seas Scrolls, and the writings of Philo and Josephus) indicate that discourse about and experience of the divine Spirit did not vanish in early Judaism. When it comes to representations of the Spirit of God, there is much continuity between Jewish scripture and tradition, on the one hand, and the letters and narratives that now compose the New Testament, on the other. To isolate the New Testament perspectives on s/Spirit from these precedents and contemporaneous cultural expressions in the Greco-Roman world is to misjudge the ways in which the experience and language of the spirit world and of the divine Spirit evident in early Christian writings participate in the wider culture.

Nevertheless, as we will discover in the following chapters, the New Testament develops Spirit talk in distinctive ways. Divine presence as (Holy) Spirit finds new company in the person of Jesus, whose mission the Spirit empowers (e.g., Luke 4:16-27; Acts 10:38). His followers continue to experience the Spirit's guidance and empowerment through his mediation (e.g., John 14:16-17, 26; 15:26; 16:7; Acts 2:33). The New Testament's notions about the supremely potent, life-giving, restoring, and community-shaping *Holy* Spirit of the one God would have resonated with and at the same time reoriented the ideas of many in the Roman Empire who heard its story. To that story, in its many variations, we now turn.

For Further Reading

Aune, David E. *Prophecy in Early Christianity and the Ancient Mediterranean World*. Grand Rapids: Eerdmans, 1983.

Engberg-Pedersen, Troels. *Cosmology and Self in the Apostle Paul: The Material Spirit*. Oxford: Oxford University Press, 2010.

Forbes, Christopher. *Prophecy and Inspired Speech in Early Christianity and Its Hellenistic Environment*. WUNT 2/75. Tübingen: Mohr Siebeck, 1995.

Holladay, Carl R. "Spirit in Philo of Alexandria." Pages 341–63 in *The Holy Spirit and the Church according to the New Testament*. Edited by Predrag Dragutinovic, Karl-Wilhelm Niebuhr, and James Buchanan Wallace. WUNT 1/354. Tübingen: Mohr Siebeck, 2016.

Isaacs, Marie E. *The Concept of the Spirit: A Study of Pneuma in Hellenistic Judaism and Its Bearing on the New Testament*. London: Heythrop College, 1976.

Levison, John R. *Filled with the Spirit*. Grand Rapids: Eerdmans, 2009.

———. *Inspired: The Holy Spirit and the Mind of Faith*. Grand Rapids: Eerdmans, 2013.

———. *The Spirit in First Century Judaism*. AGJU 29. Leiden: Brill, 1997.

Martin, Troy W. "Paul's Pneumatological Statements and Ancient Medical Texts." Pages 105–26 in *The New Testament and Early Christian Literature in Greco-Roman Context: Studies in Honor of David E. Aune*. Edited by John Fotopoulos. NovTSup 122. Leiden: Brill, 2006.

Montague, George T. *The Holy Spirit: Growth of a Biblical Tradition.* New York: Paulist, 1976.

Paige, Terence. "Who Believes in 'Spirit'? *Pneuma* in Pagan Usage and Implications for Gentile Christian Mission." *HTR* 95 (2002): 417–36.

Peppard, Michael. *The Son of God in the Roman World: Divine Sonship in Its Social and Political Context.* New York: Oxford University Press, 2011.

Rabens, Volker. "Geistes-Geschichte: Die rede vom Geist im Horizont der griechisch-römischen und jüdisch-hellenistischen Literatur." *ZNW* 25 (2010): 46–55.

Sekki, Arthur Everett. *The Meaning of Ruaḥ at Qumran.* SBLDS 110. Atlanta: Scholars Press, 1989.

Chapter 4

The Holy Spirit in Mark and Matthew

Each of the four New Testament Gospels takes note of the presence and activity of the Holy Spirit, though the variations among the accounts are fascinating and merit separate treatment of each narrative. *Mark* throws the spotlight on a fierce contest between the Spirit-authorized Messiah and unclean spirits that oppress people. Jesus also assures the disciples that when they encounter hostility in their future mission the Holy Spirit will give them a bold voice. *Matthew* adds a number of hues to the portrait: the Holy Spirit plays a direct role in connection with Jesus's birth and also with his acts of compassionate healing, pictured as the Spirit-fueled vocation of the servant of God and thus the fulfillment of prophecy. The concluding lines of the Gospel anticipate the disciples' mission teaching all nations and baptizing in the name of Father, Son, and Holy Spirit (Matt 28:19-20). In *Luke*, as in Matthew, the Holy Spirit is pictured as the source of Jesus's life—but also as the prompter for prophetic speech that seeks to make sense of the momentous events that are unfolding. Jesus also commences his ministry under the direction and empowerment of the Holy Spirit and invokes the divine Spirit to legitimate and define the content of his mission.

Luke alone among the Gospel writers continues the story of Jesus in a second narrative, the book of *Acts*, which tracks the post-Easter mission of Jesus's followers. In this narrative sequel to the Gospel, the Holy Spirit is especially prominent, cast by Luke as mission director representing God's guidance of the movement. At key junctures of transition and boundary-crossing (the inclusion of Samaritans and Gentiles), the Spirit leads the way, overcoming human inertia and resistance. So Luke tells the story of the emergence of an expanding network of inclusive communities of Jesus followers: for them, social and religious identity is defined in terms of the initiative of the Spirit rather than various cultural markers.

John offers a distinctive portrait of the Holy Spirit. In the farewell discourses in this Gospel (John 13–17), Jesus highlights the Spirit's role as *Paraclete*—an advocate, encourager, and teacher who bears witness to the truth and continues Jesus's mission of revealing the divine Father to the world.

This chapter will provide brief discussions of the Spirit in Mark and then Matthew. Chapter 5 will present a more extensive analysis of the Spirit in Luke and Acts. Chapter 6 will turn to the distinctive presentation of the Spirit in the Gospel of John.

The Gospel According to Mark

We begin exploration of Gospel views of the Holy Spirit with Mark, probably the earliest of the Gospels and perhaps the first such written account to be composed. This telling of the story suggests its setting in a time of crisis, including the experience of or potential for suffering for Jesus followers, around the time of the destruction of the Jerusalem temple in 70 CE.[1] Reflecting this setting are the urgent tone of the narrative and the intense struggle it relates between Jesus's Spirit-powered mission to advance the reign of God and the tenacious forces of evil that oppress human beings. So although there are few explicit mentions of the Holy Spirit, Mark's Gospel places in the foreground conflict between the Spirit or reign of God and the unclean and destructive spirits. In this rendition of Jesus's healing activity, his repeated moves to free people from the harmful interference of these spirits point to the potency of both the reign of God and the Holy Spirit (see, e.g., 1:14-15; 3:22-30).

The Holy Spirit makes a big initial splash in the Jordan River, as the baptizing prophet John predicts the coming of a stronger, more highly honored one who will supplant John's water baptism by baptizing in/ with the Holy Spirit (Mark 1:7-8), and in short order then baptizes Jesus (v. 9). A private revelation to Jesus in vision and voice immediately ensues: the heavens are ripped open, the Spirit descends in the manner of a dove upon him, and a voice out of the now-opened heaven affirms Jesus as the beloved divine Son (vv. 10-11). (Matt 3:17 turns this into a public disclosure, as the heavenly voice begins "This is" rather than "You are.") Does the dove symbolize that the Spirit's coming to Jesus is the "harbinger of the new world" (thus echoing Gen 8:8-12 in the flood narrative; cf. 4 Baruch 7:8)?[2] In this opening scene in which Jesus appears, the Spirit's descent associates Jesus's identity with heaven (Son of God) and prepares readers for future confrontations with unclean, demonic spirits in which Jesus will embody holy and strong (divine) presence.

In the immediate aftermath of the baptismal theophany revealing Jesus's identity, the Spirit takes a different tack: "At once the Spirit forced Jesus out into the wilderness" (Mark 1:12), where he was subjected to rigorous testing by Satan for forty days in the company of wild animals. But there he also enjoyed the supporting presence of angels (v. 13). Mark leaves as a gap to be filled by the reader the what and why of the testing by Satan, and also the motive of the Spirit in forcing Jesus into this collision with the forces of evil (the verb *forced out* [*ekballein*] is a strong one and later depicts Jesus's action toward oppressive demons; see, e.g., 1:34; 3:22-23; 7:13). This is no holiday excursion to a desert resort! The impression is clear, however, that Jesus, as the Spirit-endowed Son of God, will face intense conflict with the powers of evil but will engage that challenge with supporting divine presence. At the story's end, Jesus's robust human spirit, buoyed by the divine Spirit, will face one final ordeal: with suffering and death looming, Jesus urges his companions to remain alert and to pray as a potentially catastrophic test of their fidelity draws near, for "the spirit is eager, but the flesh is weak" (14:38). Jesus—spirit and body—will prove willing and prepared, but the disciples, who in fatigue succumb to sleep rather than pray, will be overmastered by events.

The narrative does not delay in beginning to tell of such encounters with hostile spirit-beings. After an initial declaration by Jesus that the time had arrived and God's rule was about to exert itself in the world (1:14-15), Jesus begins to recruit followers who will accompany him as disciples, as students (vv. 16-20). His first encounter with human need arises in the midst of a teaching session in a synagogue on the Sabbath, when "a person with an evil spirit" (1:23) shouts out Jesus's identity as "the holy one from God" (v. 24) and wins a swift rebuke from Jesus and an unceremonious exit (vv. 25-26). The holy one (on whom the Holy Spirit has just descended) meets a spiritual force that is un-holy and oppressive and proves himself to be the "stronger one" John had said is coming. This "new teaching" reveals extraordinary authority: "He commands even the unclean spirits and they obey him" (v. 27).

Such acts garner Jesus a rapidly spreading reputation (v. 28), and Jesus routinely bests these spirits. As participants in the spiritual realm, they are privileged to possess knowledge about Jesus's status to which humans do not yet have access (also 3:11), but they are powerless before him. He liberates persons from their harmful domination—each such act an indicator, Jesus later says, of liberation from anti-God forces (3:23-27). That assertion comes in response to detractors who allege that Jesus has power to banish demons because he is allied with Satan, the chief of demons (3:22). In such accusations, holy and unholy ("unclean spirits," "demons") are turned upside down, preventing recognition of the activity of God fostering human flourishing. This setting of sharp debate over the meaning of Jesus's assault on harmful spirits prompts him to make an enigmatic statement that has puzzled—and troubled—many readers ever since: "I assure you that human beings will be forgiven for everything, for all sins and insults of every kind. But whoever insults the Holy Spirit will never be forgiven. That person is guilty of a sin with consequences that last forever" (vv. 28-29).

The narrator explains the reason for such a stern word: "The legal experts were saying, 'He's possessed by an evil spirit'" (v. 30). Malicious slander against the Holy Spirit amounts to a willful rejection of the holy, a spurning of the activity of the holy one. Closed to God's powerful, holy presence, one is bereft of hope for the future, Jesus cautions.

Excuse Me, but Have I Committed the Unpardonable Sin?

Many people have expressed confusion and consternation about the "unpardonable sin" mentioned in Mark 3:29:

> Whoever insults the Holy Spirit will never be forgiven. That person is guilty of a sin with consequences that last forever.

Guilty as charged?

The worried self-questioning underlying the question suggests an openness to the divine presence that fits neither the circumstance assumed in this passage nor the sharp warning that Jesus issues to his critics. They are labeling actions that foster human flourishing as evil.

The juxtaposition in this passage between the Holy Spirit and the spirits implies that Jesus's campaign to free people from the destructive domination of unclean spirits is an aggressive assault against the anti-God powers over which Satan is preeminent. It is a key dimension of the working of God's powerful reign, unleashed now in Jesus's public activity in and around Galilee. There is no further mention of the Holy Spirit, though, until Jesus's teaching session in the Jerusalem temple, just prior to his arrest. Although he has ridden into the city to royal acclaim befitting a descendant of David (11:9-10), he questions the tradition of scripture interpretation that identifies the Messiah as David's son (12:35). Jesus invokes David's own testimony (assuming that the voice heard in the book of Psalms belongs to David) that the LORD (= God) addressed the Messiah as Lord (v. 36). The lower-status son of David cannot be his higher-status Lord (v. 37). Mark has Jesus credit this view of the Messiah (as Lord superior to David) to the psalmist's inspiration "by the Holy Spirit." As we will discover, Luke in particular builds on this picture of the Holy Spirit as speaking through the words of scripture. However, it takes a discerning interpreter—in this case, Jesus, but in Acts, typically Peter or Paul—to read the Spirit's teaching in scripture wisely.

A final reference in Mark to the Holy Spirit holds in prospect the disciples' future mission "to all nations" as witnesses to the good news (Mark 13:10). This mission will occur in the context of intense opposition, peril, and even persecution (13:9-13). When the disciples face adversarial judicial processes because of their commitment as Jesus followers, they will not be left to their own resources: "When they haul you in and hand you over, don't worry ahead of time about what to answer or say. Instead, say whatever is given to you at that moment, for you aren't doing the speaking but the Holy Spirit is" (v. 11). God's presence as Spirit will tutor and guide the courageous witness of God's people. Again on this point Luke, especially, will elaborate (e.g., Luke 21:12-19, a set of promises repeatedly enacted in Acts). So while Mark does not, like Luke, narrate the actualization of John's prediction that Jesus would baptize in/with the Holy Spirit (Mark 1:8), Mark's audience is assured that the effects of that Spirit-baptism will empower them for mission despite opposition. Their experience will confirm that the Holy Spirit "equips believers to confront hostile powers as they proclaim and demonstrate the reign of God."[3]

The Gospel According to Matthew

Matthew takes up each of the references to the Holy Spirit in Mark's Gospel, tweaking here and there in interesting ways and adding distinctive new features. Most scholars think Matthew's Gospel builds on Mark and a collection of Jesus's teaching shared with Luke, supplementing these sources with additional traditions and merging them in a more systematic narrative that organizes the account of Jesus's ministry around five (or six) major teaching discourses.

Jesus the Teacher: Discourses in Matthew

Sermon on the Mount: call to a life of radical righteousness (5:1–7:27)

Instruction for the disciples' mission (10:5-42)

Parables about the reign of God (13:3-52)

Practical wisdom shaping the community of disciples (18:1-35)

How not to lead: indictment of scribes and Pharisees (23:1-39)

Pictures of end-time judgment and deliverance (24:3–25:46)

The narrative was likely composed in the last third of the first century CE for Christian-Jewish groups that were engaged in vigorous debate with other Jews over fundamental questions of Jewish identity in relation to the claim that Jesus is the Messiah. In this conflicted setting Matthew seeks to make a convincing case that Jesus is the Messiah who brings Israel's history and hopes to fulfillment.[4] We will first discuss Matthew's incorporation of Markan materials on the Spirit and then conclude the chapter by exploring the distinctive Matthean expansions.

Jesus's Ministry and the Holy Spirit: Taking Cues from Mark

As in Mark, the introduction to Jesus's public career profiles the baptizing prophet John. First, though, Matthew prefaces that scene with a list of Jesus's ancestors (1:2-17) and an account of his birth, the family's flight to Egypt to avoid King Herod's rage, and his return after the fashion of another "son of God" (i.e., Israel: Hos 11:1, quoted in Matt 2:15). John announces the coming of a "stronger" one who "will baptize you with the Holy Spirit and with fire" (3:11). Verse 12 indicates that the fire baptism John imagines is one of judgment ("the chaff he will burn with unquenchable fire"), but the Spirit-baptism is the positive side of that coin, a gathering of wheat into the barn. So the image of baptism here prepares for the theme of judgment—pictured as God's separation of good and bad—that dominates the ensuing narrative (e.g., 7:15-23; 13:24-30, 36-43, 47-50; 25:31-46).

Overcoming John's reluctance to baptize a worthier person than himself, Jesus convinces John that this is the way "to fulfill all righteousness" (3:15). This detail is present only in Matthew and is another prominent concern in Matthew's story. As Jesus emerges from the water, "Heaven was opened to him, and he saw the Spirit of God coming down like a dove and resting on him" (v. 16). The voice from heaven that accompanies this visionary experience, addressed to Jesus ("you") in Mark 1:11, offers this revelation publicly in Matthew: "This is my Son, the Beloved, with whom I am well pleased" (3:17 NRSV). Readers are cued to expect that the mission Jesus is about to undertake will be that of God's beloved Son in whom the Holy Spirit, symbolized as a dove, has taken up residence. Again as in Mark—though more expansively with the report of a debate in which Jesus and the devil contest each other's interpretations of scripture (4:2-13)—the very Spirit that has conveyed divine endorsement of Jesus leads him out to the Judean desert to confront the devil's testing. A subtle variation in wording makes explicit that the Spirit is acting precisely *for the purpose of* confronting Jesus with this vocational testing (4:1). Even God's holy, righteous, beloved Son must choose well in a moral arena that includes other enticing, but unfaithful, options.

In Matthew 10, the second of the major teaching discourses Jesus delivers, he commissions twelve disciples for mission on his behalf and predicts the experiences they will eventually face, notably hostility from and accountability to governing powers (amplifying the picture in Mark 13:9-13). Jesus conveys to the Twelve power like his to heal and to liberate persons from domination by unclean spirits (Matt 10:1; Jesus's power over unclean spirits, or demons, as in 8:16). So in the healing activity of his followers, as in his own, the Spirit will best the spirits, and so foster human flourishing. But when they find themselves "haul[ed] . . . in front of" the governing powers (10:17-18), they will be aided by a divine tutor in framing the right testimony: "Whenever they hand you over, don't worry about how to speak or what you will say, because what you can say will be given to you at that moment. You aren't doing the talking, but the Spirit of my Father is doing the talking through you" (vv. 19-20). God-present-as-Spirit will prove to be a supporting Father not only to the beloved Messiah-Son of God but also to other sons (and daughters).

Building on Mark 3:22-30, Matthew shows Jesus on the defensive, countering accusations that his acts of demon expulsion attest his alliance with anti-God powers. He is accused of drawing his remarkable power from the ruler of demons (Matt 12:22-32). Actually, Jesus reads their thoughts (v. 25) and then goes on the offensive. Point one: common sense refutes his critics' charge, for a kingdom or a house divided (Satan's too!) will fall (vv. 25-26). Point two: does anyone accuse other Jewish exorcists of tapping demonic power to defeat demons (v. 27)? And decisive point three: "But if I throw out demons by the power of God's Spirit, then God's kingdom has already overtaken you" (v. 28). That is, in Jesus's acts of kingdom power, the strong man (Satan) has been bound and his property (persons dominated by demons) removed from his possession (v. 29). Jesus points to his acts of healing and releasing people from oppression by unclean spirits as evidence that the powerful reign of God is exerting itself in the presence of his audience. As we will soon see, the preceding passage (12:15-21) also marks this healing ministry as a pointer to Jesus's role as the servant of God, in fulfillment of the prophecy of Isaiah.

Following the pattern in Mark 3:22-30, Matthew places the difficult saying of Jesus about inexcusable slander against the Holy Spirit in the setting of sharp debate about the meaning of Jesus's acts of demon expulsion (Matt 12:31-32). If Jesus does what he does by empowerment from the Holy Spirit, and if the results so obviously bring benefit to human beings, the persistent labeling of that work as evil and anti-God amounts to a turn away from holy divine presence, which is reclaiming the world for God's governance. There is irony here: by speaking against the Spirit present in Jesus's ministry, one rejects a mission that had as its very purpose rescue from the destructive consequence of sins (1:21). So one places oneself beyond the reach of forgiveness.[5] This pattern is reminiscent of the grieving of God's Spirit in Isaiah 63:10, where the people have rebelled against God despite the experience of divine deliverance and care.[6] God's saving presence thus becomes enmity.

Finally, as in Mark's Gospel, Matthew embeds in a series of vigorous exchanges between Jesus and other teachers/leaders in the Jerusalem temple a provocative barrage of rhetorical questions that seem to carry the implication that the Messiah is David's son (Matt 22:41-45). Again, David's voice in Psalm 110:1 is said to be Spirit-inspired (Matt 22:43). The episode ends with the report that these words of Jesus reduce his listeners to silence (v. 46, relocated from its Markan position at the close of the preceding conversation, Mark 12:28-34). Matthew's readers may be puzzled as well, for this apparent debunking of the Messiah's Davidic lineage contradicts the Gospel's presentation of Jesus the Messiah as David's son, beginning with the genealogy of 1:2-17. Reading from the end of the story backward, the Matthean audience will be able to see *how* the Messiah can be David's son and also his Lord: God's raising of Jesus will confirm his superior status and honor. For now, Jesus may have silenced his detractors; however, he does not keep quiet, as Matthew 23 proceeds to address to the crowds a harsh rebuke of the conduct of the scribes and Pharisees. Their hostility toward Jesus will subsequently take more indirect channels. In the rest of the chapter, we explore dimensions of Matthew's profile of the Holy Spirit that represent a deepening of the Markan portrait.

"Pregnant by the Holy Spirit": God-Present in Matthew 1:18-23 and 28:18-20

In a move also made by Luke, Matthew draws the Holy Spirit into an active role already at the beginning of Jesus's life. Twice accenting that Mary has "become pregnant by the Holy Spirit" (1:18, 20), Matthew locates the origin of Jesus's life in God. Countering the seeming indicators that this birth is the result of shameful conduct that deprives Mary of honor, Matthew surrounds the incongruity of Mary's pregnancy with emblems of honor. Righteous Joseph has a dream in which he hears a message from heaven that reframes his understanding of what is happening: the son to whom she will give birth "was conceived by the Holy Spirit" (v. 20), and, bearing the name Jesus, he "will save his people from their sins" (v. 21)—thus fulfilling the prophetic promise: "'Look, the virgin shall conceive and bear a son, and they shall name him Emmanuel,' which means, 'God is with us'" (v. 23). A holy child whose origins lie in the Holy Spirit will bring forgiveness to the people and will embody divine, holy presence. As Schweizer puts it, the story of the virgin birth (more accurately, conception) is "an ambiguous sign that over Jesus' birth hovers a direct act of the Creator."[7] Matthew goes to considerable lengths, however, to remove the ambiguity: dream-revelation, scripture perceptively interpreted, and the meaning of a name (or two: Jesus and Emmanuel) converge to locate Jesus's very life within the creative-redemptive working of God.

Returning to the image of God-present, the end of the narrative frames the whole story with the affirmation of divine presence through Jesus (28:20; cf. 18:20). God-present "with us" (Emmanuel), Holy Spirit as God-present in Jesus, and Jesus-present "with you": thus the narrative Matthew composes prepares for a closing mandate to the disciples to baptize in the threefold name of Father, Son, and Holy Spirit (28:19). There is no full-blown doctrine of the Trinity already in Matthew's Gospel, but this liturgical formula certainly anticipates later theological developments.

Spirited Servant: Matthew 12:15-21

Matthew accents not only Jesus's teaching authority and message but also his activity as compassionate healer, supplementing numerous individual healing episodes with no fewer than ten general summaries by the narrator.[8] Twice the narrator presents Jesus's healing ministry as the realization of the prophetic paradigm of the servant of the Lord in Second Isaiah (a portion of the book of Isaiah that comes from the period of the Exile, chs. 40–55). In Matthew 8:17 Jesus is said to fulfill the role of the servant in Isaiah 53:4, who bears in himself the infirmities and diseases of his people.

In Matthew 12:15-21 Jesus's acts of healing, and especially his attempts to enforce silence about them, are interpreted as the fulfillment of Isaiah 42:1-4:

> [This happened] so that what was spoken through Isaiah the prophet might be fulfilled: "Look, my Servant whom I chose, the one I love, in whom I find great pleasure. I'll put my Spirit upon him, and he'll announce judgment to the Gentiles. He won't argue or shout, and nobody will hear his voice in the streets. He won't break a bent stalk, and he won't snuff out a smoldering wick, until he makes justice win. And the Gentiles will put their hope in his name." (Matt 12:17-21)

Three details in this lengthy quotation from Isaiah 42 are striking. First, echoing the account of Jesus's baptism, the passage pictures Jesus as acted upon by God's Spirit (Matt 12:18; the words "the one I love [*agapētos*]" and "in whom I find great pleasure [*eudokēsen*]" also recall 3:17). The divine Spirit is thus the source of Jesus's ability to heal and, in the accent of this passage, the Spirit is the source of the justice and hope Jesus delivers. The Spirit is present and active in Jesus's speaking and healing.

Second, it is Gentiles, in particular, to whom Jesus conveys these benefits (vv. 18, 21; 4:12-16 also associates the region of Galilee with Gentiles). This is a remarkable reading of Jewish scripture in a Gospel that is dominated by concerns about Jewish identity and about legitimate interpretations of the Torah and the Prophets, and in which Jesus's ministry with few exceptions is restricted to fellow Jews (note his statement of mission principle in 10:5-6; 15:24). However, the motif anticipates Jesus's final words to the disciples, which dispatch them to all nations (or Gentiles, *panta ta ethnē* in 28:19).

Third, although the narrative setting places acts of healing in the foreground, the quotation from Isaiah emphasizes "justice" (or "judgment," *krisis*). This is a prominent concern in Matthew (*krisis* in 10:15; 11:22, 24; 12:41-42; 23:23; and repeatedly, without the word, judgment in the form of separation between good and bad). As in 8:10-13 and 11:20-24, outsiders are given hope—justice, therefore, in a positive sense. Insiders, though (in 11:20-24, the Galilean towns of Chorazin, Bethsaida, and Capernaum), face judgment—justice in a negative sense—because of their failure to realign life to the claims and commitments of God's realm, even in the light of Jesus's powerful acts of healing. Matthew thus appropriates the prophetic text from Isaiah 42 to portray Jesus as empowered by the Spirit to convey the reality of justice/judgment in its positive and negative aspects. Whether this *krisis* is a positive outcome depends on the response of those who listen to Jesus's message and those who observe his acts of healing and liberation.

In closing our study of the Holy Spirit in Matthew, a brief comment on Matthew's account of Jesus's dying breath may be useful. In a manner similar to John 19:30, Matthew employs spirit language in connection with the death of Jesus: "Then Jesus cried again with a loud voice and breathed his last [or gave up his spirit, *pneuma*]" (Matt 27:50 NRSV). His life began in a creative act of the Holy Spirit (1:20), and in the scene of his baptism-anointing readers witnessed the descent of the Spirit of God and its coming upon him (3:16). Now, he releases the s/Spirit as he dies. His future (resurrection) life will entail a fresh creative, life-imparting act of God. Thereafter, he will send the disciples out to baptize in (Father, Son, and) Spirit—not exactly the Pentecost explosion of Acts 2, but an effective witness, nonetheless, to the continuing power of Jesus's followers to teach, heal, and welcome into community any and all.

For Further Reading

Black, C. Clifton. *Mark*. ANTC. Nashville: Abingdon, 2011.

Boring, M. Eugene. *Mark: A Commentary*. NTL. Louisville: Westminster John Knox, 2006.

Carroll, John T. *Jesus and the Gospels: An Introduction*. Louisville: Westminster John Knox, 2016.

Carter, Warren. *Matthew and the Margins: A Sociopolitical and Religious Reading*. Maryknoll, NY: Orbis Books, 2000.

Charette, Blaine. *Restoring Presence: The Spirit in Matthew's Gospel*. JPTSup 18. Sheffield: Sheffield Academic, 2000.

Keener, Craig S. *The Spirit in the Gospels and Acts: Divine Purity and Power*. Peabody, MA: Hendrickson, 1997. Repr., Grand Rapids: Baker, 2010.

Levison, John R. *Filled with the Spirit*. Grand Rapids: Eerdmans, 2009.

———. *Inspired: The Holy Spirit and the Mind of Faith*. Grand Rapids: Eerdmans, 2013.

Schweizer, Eduard. *The Holy Spirit*. Translated by Reginald H. Fuller and Ilse Fuller. Philadelphia: Fortress, 1980.

Senior, Donald. *The Gospel of Matthew*. IBT. Nashville: Abingdon, 1997.

———. *Matthew*. ANTC. Nashville: Abingdon, 1998.

Chapter 5

The Holy Spirit in Luke-Acts

Luke's Gospel and the book of Acts together form a two-volume narrative, the first book (the Gospel) relating the ministry of Jesus and the second (Acts) continuing the story by tracing the early mission of his followers, especially Simon Peter and then Paul. Each volume features an inaugural speech that sets forth the basic pattern and program of the ensuing narrative. In the Gospel, a career-opening episode in Nazareth presents Jesus's mission statement and the hostile reception it provokes (Luke 4:16-30). In Acts, the inaugural moment features Peter's Pentecost sermon (Acts 2:14-36). Each of these programmatic speeches assigns a decisive role to the Holy Spirit: first the ministry of Jesus and then that of his followers represent the fulfillment of ancient promises of God's dynamic presence:

> [Jesus says:] "The Spirit of the Lord is upon me, because the Lord has anointed me. He has sent me to preach good news to the poor, to proclaim release to the prisoners and recovery of sight to the blind, to liberate the oppressed, and to proclaim the year of the Lord's favor." . . . Today, this scripture has been fulfilled just as you heard it. (Luke 4:18-19, 21, quoting lines from Isa 61:1-2 and 58:6)

> [Peter says:] This is what was spoken through the prophet Joel: "In the last days," God says, "I will pour out my Spirit on all people. Your sons and daughters will prophesy. Your young will see visions. Your elders will

dream dreams. Even upon my servants, men and women, I will pour out my Spirit in those days, and they will prophesy....And everyone who calls on the name of the Lord will be saved."...Change your hearts and lives. Each of you must be baptized in the name of Jesus Christ for the forgiveness of your sins. Then you will receive the gift of the Holy Spirit. This promise is for you, your children, and for all who are far away—as many as the Lord our God invites (Acts 2:16-21, 38-39, quoting Joel 2:28-32 = LXX 3:1-5)

The Spirit will guide and empower both Jesus's mission to restore God's people Israel and the apostles' mission to continue that project and to extend God's blessing to all peoples and nations—all in fulfillment of scriptural promise. The Holy Spirit places a divine signature on the activity of Jesus and the apostles.

The Gospel According to Luke

Even before Jesus launches his mission in Nazareth by claiming that the divine Spirit has specially chosen ("anointed") and commissioned him, the Holy Spirit is a prominent player in Luke 1:5–4:15. When the heavenly messenger Gabriel announces to the skeptical, aging priest Zechariah that he and his wife, Elizabeth, would become parents, he forecasts a future role for their son-to-be, John, as a Spirit-filled prophet (1:15). Indeed, he will be Spirit-filled even before birth, a prediction that soon finds dramatic fulfillment in the encounter between Elizabeth and Mary, mother-to-be of Jesus (1:44, though here John's leap within his mother's womb receives prophetic interpretation in the voice of Elizabeth). The divine Spirit not only prompts prophetic activity, but also acts to bring the Messiah into the world. Gabriel, revealing to an unmarried Mary that she would give birth to a special son, explains how this marvel is possible: "The Holy Spirit will come over you and the power of the Most High will overshadow you. Therefore, the one who is to be born will be holy. He will be called God's Son" (1:35). The point is not that the divine Spirit substitutes for a biological father and contributes a share of the genetic makeup of Jesus. Rather, the Holy Spirit's association with Jesus's birth signifies that his life has its origin in God. He is holy as Son of the God who is holy.

His arrival means that God is acting in fulfillment of the ancient promise (e.g., 2 Sam 7:12-13).

Especially prominent in Luke 1–2 is the image of the Holy Spirit animating and informing prophetic interpretation of the momentous events being narrated. Zechariah, father of the newborn prophet-to-be John the Baptizer, delivers an inspired hymn-oracle in praise of God, whose saving intervention in Israel's history is now underway (1:68-79). The narrator labels the hymn *prophecy* and indicates that Zechariah's prophetic message results from his being "filled with the Holy Spirit" (v. 67). As Luke's second book will also make clear, among the signs of the Spirit's presence is the gift of prophetic insight and speech, pointing to God's activity in the world, and realizing the scriptural promise (Acts 2:17-21).

Spirit-animated prophetic activity resumes after the birth of Jesus, when the Holy Spirit rests on the devout man Simeon and guides his steps so that he encounters the infant boy and his parents (Mary and Joseph) in the temple (Luke 2:25-27). Holding the baby in his arms (v. 28), Simeon proceeds to offer a hybrid prayer-prophetic oracle that celebrates God's provision of salvation encompassing all peoples—glory/honor for Israel and illuminating revelation for Gentiles (or the nations, *ethnē*, vv. 29-32). But there will also be resistance and division (vv. 34-35). Simeon's Spirit-directed speech lays out much of the plot and program of Luke's ensuing narrative.

Luke 3 brings the adult Jesus on the scene and the divine Spirit accompanies him, even through a forty-day ordeal of vocational testing in the wilderness. Jesus accepts ritual washing (baptism), signaling his solidarity with the prophet John's summons to the people to reorient life around the promise of God's reign. Indeed, without yet knowing the identity of the person in view, John pointed in advance beyond his own water-baptism ritual to the coming of a stronger one who would baptize with the Holy Spirit and fire (3:16). The Holy Spirit makes a dramatic appearance on the occasion: "When... Jesus also was baptized [and] was praying, heaven was opened and the Holy Spirit came down on him in bodily form like a dove. And there was a voice from heaven: 'You are my Son, whom I dearly love; in you I find happiness'" (3:21-22). Sound and sight join forces to trumpet Jesus's special status: heaven opens, the divine voice affirms Jesus as beloved Son of God, and the Holy Spirit places a personal stamp on him, symbolically represented in the descent of a dove.

Spirit and Dove

Luke's account of the baptism of Jesus highlights the Holy Spirit's descent "in bodily form like a dove" (3:22). What is the significance of the dove?

Among the proposals are the following:

Spirit is like a bird soaring over the waters in the world's creation (Gen 1:2) – but no bird is mentioned in the text!

Spirit as dove recalls the new beginning and restoration after the flood (Gen 8:8).

Spirit-dove is a bird omen symbolizing the peaceful mission of this Son of God, in contrast to the eagle as image of Roman military domination (Peppard, *Son of God*, 115–23).

But what does it mean to be a Spirit-anointed Son of God? Jesus is not left to his own devices to figure it out. Mentions of the Spirit frame the wilderness testing in which Jesus considers what kind of Messiah he is called to be (4:2-13):

Jesus returned from the Jordan River full of the Holy Spirit, and was led by the Spirit into the wilderness. (4:1)

Jesus returned in the power of the Spirit to Galilee, and news about him spread throughout the whole countryside. He taught in their synagogues and was praised by everyone. (4:14-15)

"Full of the Holy Spirit," "led by the Spirit," and "in the power of the Spirit," Jesus is able to discern what his vocation entails, and he undertakes it as the agent of God's dynamic presence in Israel's story. His mission begins under the direction and empowerment of God's Spirit-presence. So Luke prepares for the programmatic episode in Jesus's hometown Nazareth, where he appeals to the prophet Isaiah (61:1-2 and 58:6) to unveil his ministry's core commitments and activities as a Spirit-anointed and Spirit-empowered leader (4:18-21). The Spirit has commissioned him to declare good news to the poor and to liberate people from all manner of confining and oppressive conditions.

After this initial "big splash" of Spirit activity as Jesus comes on the scene, Luke's narrative makes only a few mentions of the Holy Spirit—until book two, when the Spirit plays a prominent role as the mission director for Jesus's followers. But the Holy Spirit's emphatic intervention at the beginning of Jesus's career will incline readers to view his subsequent work as also Spirit-fueled.

Luke's story often depicts Jesus engaged in prayer, and typically at key moments of revelation, decision, and action (3:21-22; 6:12; 9:18, 28; 11:1; 22:39-46; 23:34, 46). On one such occasion, the disciples ask Jesus to instruct them in the art of prayer, and he obliges by giving a model prayer (11:2-4). The mini-parable and sayings that follow highlight the importance of trust in a generous God, on which prayer rests (vv. 5-13). Jesus urges listeners to (continually and insistently) ask, seek, and knock, expecting that they will receive, find, and gain access (vv. 9-10). A lesser-to-greater argument in verses 11-13 offers the generous provision of human parents for their children (ordinarily but not always, we are well aware!) as reason for confidence in God: "If you who are evil know how to give good gifts to your children, how much more will the heavenly Father give the Holy Spirit to those who ask him?" (v. 13).

A side glance at Matthew turns up a small but meaningful variation: while the parallel saying in Matthew 7:11 depicts the heavenly Father giving *good things* to those who ask, Luke has Jesus promise the *Holy Spirit*. What better answer to prayer, especially for persons experiencing difficulty and distress, than the empowering, strengthening, reassuring presence of God?

Ask, and You Will Be Given ... the Holy Spirit

Matthew 7:11

If you who are evil know how to give good gifts to your children, how much more will your heavenly Father give good things to those who ask him.

Luke 11:13

If you who are evil know how to give good gifts to your children, how much more will the heavenly Father give the Holy Spirit to those who ask him?

In Luke 12:8-12 Jesus assures his followers that when they are called to give testimony before hostile authorities in their future mission, the Holy Spirit will accompany them as tutor and encourager under duress: "When they bring you before the synagogues, rulers, and authorities, don't worry about how to defend yourself or what you should say. The Holy Spirit will tell you at that very moment what you must say" (vv. 11-12). Indeed, Jesus issues a stern warning to anyone who slanders their Spirit-inspired testimony: "Anyone who speaks a word against the Human One will be forgiven, but whoever insults the Holy Spirit won't be forgiven" (v. 10). Jesus's promise of Spirit empowerment for witness, despite opposition, is repeatedly enacted in the book of Acts (e.g., Acts 2:17-36; also, note the prayer and its outcome in courageous, Spirit-inspired witness in Acts 4:29-31).

Anticipation of that mission by Jesus's followers becomes fervent as readers come to the end of Luke's Gospel. Jesus, crucified by order of the governor Pilate (though he repeatedly declares him unjustly charged: Luke 23:4, 14, 22), has died, surrendering his life breath-spirit (*pneuma*) to God (23:46, quoting Ps 31:6). But on Easter he appears a number of times to his closest followers, and in his final words to them he pledges to send them the "promise of the Father," which will empower them for their role as witnesses on his behalf (Luke 24:48-49). The narrative sequel will not delay long in disclosing to readers that the power for mission that will come to the disciples will be the Holy Spirit (the Pentecost story in Acts 2).

The Acts of the Apostles

So prominent is the Holy Spirit in Acts that it has aptly been labeled the "Book of the Holy Spirit."[1] In Luke's second volume, the word *pneuma* (s/Spirit) appears seventy times! Eight of these refer to evil or unclean spirits, or to a "pythonic spirit" (spirit of divination: 16:16-19), and four to the human spirit, but the other fifty-eight references are to the Holy Spirit or Spirit of God (Spirit of Christ as a synonymous expression in 16:7). We focus attention in this section on the various ways in which the divine Spirit figures in the Acts narrative.

The Spirit is often depicted in Acts as a force that "fills" people and that influences or empowers human speech and action. Jesus's followers are able to speak with boldness, persuasive eloquence, and prophetic insight because the Spirit equips them (e.g., Acts 2:4; 4:31; 19:6). Thus the Spirit can be a gift that is given (10:45; 15:8), and both God and Jesus are said to provide this gift (2:33; 15:8; cf. 21:11). Moreover, the Spirit is pictured as speaking to characters within the story, and thus to readers, through the text of scripture, whether the voice belongs to the "David" of the Psalms (1:16; 4:25) or to Isaiah (28:25). On occasion people resist or oppose the Spirit (5:3, 9; 7:51).

What Does the Spirit Do in Acts?

As a character in the Acts narrative, the Spirit:

speaks

hinders speech

directs or hinders movement

descends or comes upon people

Frequently the Holy Spirit is a distinct character, a personal agent in the narrative who speaks (e.g., 8:29; 10:19; 11:12; 13:2; cf. 20:23) or hinders speech (16:6), directs or hinders movement (8:39; 13:4; 16:7 [Spirit of Jesus]; 20:22; cf. 21:4), and falls or comes upon people (1:8; 2:3; 10:44; 11:15).[2] Throughout Acts, when the Spirit appears as a distinct character, it is not as an independent actor but as the agent and representative of God (or, in 16:7, of Christ). The Holy Spirit can be aligned with or partner to human faith (6:5; 11:24), wisdom/discernment (6:3, 10; 15:28), and joy (13:52). The linkage intimates that the divine Spirit is the source of these human qualities. Far from being simply the cause of ecstatic gifts such as speaking in other languages, the Holy Spirit in Acts is evident in the core activities of effective mission, including wise discernment, bold proclamation, and openness to welcome of others who are ethnically and culturally "other."[3]

What Does the Spirit in Acts Equip People to Be and Do?

Qualities resulting from the operation of the Spirit in Acts:

bold, persuasive speech

prophetic insight

faith

wisdom and discernment

joy

welcoming persons who are ethnically or culturally "other"

Acts is the "book of the Spirit" because the story it tells is the story of God's saving activity in Israel and among all people, and often the Spirit is the character through whom God carries out this activity and moves people to participate in it. The Holy Spirit is therefore a major factor in the expansion of the movement that Luke likes to call the Way (9:2; 19:9, 23; 22:4; 24:14, 22). This mode of divine presence equips and empowers Jesus's followers for their mission "to the end of the earth" (1:8) and, especially at critical junctures of transition, guides the movement to welcome people across accepted social-cultural boundaries (Samaritans in 8:4-17 and Gentiles in 10:1-48).

The beginning of Acts recalls "what the Father had promised" (1:4), the power from on high mentioned in Jesus's last words in the Gospel (Luke 24:49). The risen Jesus explicitly identifies this divinely promised power as the Holy Spirit (Acts 1:8). Jesus also pictures this imminent gift of Spirit-power as the baptism in/with the Holy Spirit that John had predicted the coming Messiah would bring (1:5, recalling Luke 3:16, though the quote is not exact). The images of baptism, Spirit, and witness/conversion will appear together (sometimes also with laying on of hands), with fascinating variations in sequence, at several places in the ensuing narrative. Key in the narrative (as signaled in Acts 1:7-8, echoing Luke 24:48-49) is the connection between Spirit-power and the witness to all peoples that is the primary vocation of the apostles and their band.

The Holy Spirit in Acts: Prompt for Prophetic Speech and Interpretation

As we have seen, the opening chapters of Luke's Gospel highlight the Holy Spirit's activity informing and inspiring prophetic proclamation. Acts picks up this thread, beginning in the pivotal Pentecost scene of chapter 2. A crowd presumably numbering about 120 disciples gather within an upstairs room in Jerusalem. (They form a company of ten for each of the twelve apostles; for the number, see 1:15). The narrator reports that they are "filled with the Holy Spirit" (2:4). The result is that they are able to communicate their message about "the mighty works of God" (v. 11) so that people representing a dozen or more language groups are able to understand. The Spirit empowers effective speech across cultural and linguistic borders. Some listeners are skeptical, however, and in response to their charge that the Jesus followers are simply drunk Simon Peter gives an eloquent speech, its essential arguments captured in verses 14-40. Although Peter's message is not explicitly credited to Spirit inspiration, that is a reasonable inference in light of the preceding verses. Thoughtful interpretation and the prompting of the Spirit go hand in glove to inform proclamation. Spirit-inspired proclamation builds on perceptive interpretation—of recent and current events in light of scripture, and of scripture in light of recent and current events.

Speaking in Tongues: Acts 2 and 1 Corinthians 12–14

Both Acts and Paul depict unusual speech "in tongues" as a result of the Holy Spirit's influence. Are they describing the same phenomenon? The contrasts are revealing:

In 1 Corinthians, the meaning of the tongues-talk is unknown to speaker and listener alike, unless someone (also Spirit-prompted!) provides a prophetic interpretation of the message.

In Acts 2, the meaning and message of the speaker are clearly understood—and by persons who hear the message in their own languages. Here, the speaking in tongues is itself a form of prophetic interpretation.

Peter's first move in the speech is to explain the spirited talk of the believers: it is not a sign of drunkenness but the fulfillment of the prophecy of Joel:

> In the last days, God says, I will pour out my Spirit on all people. Your sons and daughters will prophesy. Your young will see visions. Your elders will dream dreams. Even upon my servants, men and women, I will pour out my Spirit in those days, and they will prophesy....And everyone who calls on the name of the Lord will be saved. (2:17-18, 21; this and the omitted lines quote with some adaptation from Joel 2:28-32 = LXX 3:1-5)

Beginning with this very speech, Jesus's followers become Spirit-guided prophetic speakers whose words move many listeners to "call on the name of the Lord." Peter promises his audience that the gift of the Spirit will not be restricted but will instead be available to all who repent, receive baptism "in the name of Jesus Christ," and obtain forgiveness (Acts 2:38). There will be more Pentecost-like events as the narrative unfolds.

The passage from Joel, which Peter quotes at some length, emphasizes that the gift of the Spirit will inspire visionary thinking and perceptive prophetic speech in young and old, male and female. The role of prophet—and equipping for the role provided by the Spirit—belongs to the whole community. The ensuing narrative will give a hint of the fulfillment of this prediction, with frequent notice of dreams, visions, and bold prophetic speech, as well as mention of the prophetic activity of four daughters of the evangelist Philip (though their words are not reported; 21:9). But only a hint of fulfillment, as full realization of the promise will lie beyond the story Luke tells:

> Although this vision hardly materializes in the book of Acts, where Luke's attention tends to be riveted instead upon an authoritative group of male leaders, such a vision of an ecstatic and inexplicably intelligent band of slaves, women, and aged, lies nonetheless at the heart of what it meant to be filled with the holy spirit.[4]

Within Luke's narrative, the Holy Spirit informs, energizes, and emboldens proclamation and witness.[5] Courageous witness it must be, as Spirit-led speakers on occasion meet stiff opposition. Peter, already arrested for what the local ruling elite in Jerusalem consider troublesome teaching about resurrection, is "inspired by the Holy Spirit" (4:8) and persists in his courageous witness to the one Lord who can save—a dig at the imperial propaganda in behalf of the emperor (4:1-12). Under threat in Jerusalem therefore, as Jesus had been, his followers recall the events that had brought "Herod and Pontius Pilate, with Gentiles and Israelites" against Jesus (4:27). They interpret these recent events as prophesied by "the Holy Spirit through" King David (4:25-26, quoting from Ps 2:1-2), whose voice they believe they hear in the psalm. In the setting of grave peril to the community of Jesus followers now, they pray for boldness to continue to speak their message (Acts 4:29). The divine answer to this petition is swift: "After they prayed, the place where they were gathered was shaken. They were all filled with the Holy Spirit and began speaking God's word with confidence" (4:31). The Holy Spirit empowers articulate, bold witness, just as Jesus had promised (Luke 12:11-12; cf. 11:13; 21:15).

Shortly afterward, Stephen speaks with such "wisdom the Spirit gave him" that his detractors cannot match or defeat him (Acts 6:10): again, fulfillment of Jesus's promise. Stephen's provocative "defense" speech, though, does result in his death at the hands of a mob—but not before the narrator observes that, "filled with the Holy Spirit," Stephen sees "the glory of God and Jesus standing at the right hand of God" (7:55 NRSV). Moreover, like Jesus before him (Luke 23:34), he is able to ask for mercy for his enemies (Acts 7:60).

Danger follows Paul throughout his Spirit-directed (9:17) mission, and intensifies as he comes to Jerusalem for the final time. The Spirit prompts prophets to speak up, warning Paul of the ominous reception ahead: "Compelled by the Spirit, they kept telling Paul not to go to Jerusalem" (21:4). A prophet named Agabus also joins the chorus of warning: "This is what the Holy Spirit says: 'In Jerusalem the Jews will bind the man who owns this belt, and they will hand him over to the Gentiles'" (21:11). What ensues is intriguing: confronted by Spirit-inspired predictions, "we and the local believers urged Paul not to go up to Jerusalem" (v. 12). The Spirit speaks, but not in a way that overrides thoughtful discernment, compels acquiescence, or ensures agreement in the group. As it turns out, however, Paul expresses willingness to face the suffering and even death that may await him in Jerusalem (v. 13). And "since we couldn't talk him out of it, the only thing we could say was, 'The Lord's will be done'" (v. 14). Indeed: God's purpose directs the story and its outcome, which will bring arrest but not death to Paul in Jerusalem. Bold witness in Rome beckons and will end the narrative (28:14-31).

The Holy Spirit in Acts: Mission Director

Jesus's final words in the Gospel set the stage for an ambitious mission to be undertaken by his followers. They would bring "to all nations" a message of "a change of heart and life for the forgiveness of sins," extended through the crucified and risen Messiah, with Jerusalem as the launching pad (Luke 24:47). As Acts tells the story of this mission, there is no doubt about who is in charge. The power from on high (Luke 24:49; Acts 1:8) not only inspires and informs prophetic speech but also charts the course for Jesus's followers. They follow the Spirit's lead. God is in charge, and from Pentecost onward, the Holy Spirit is the mission director.[6]

Three passages illustrate this important theme. The story of Saul's transformation in Acts 9 is one of dramatic reversal. This rageful enemy of the movement (8:1-3; 9:1-2) is recruited from the ranks of the opposition and soon becomes a vigorous proponent. It takes a remarkable encounter with the risen Lord, however, to redirect Saul (from ch. 13 onward called Paul) for a new mission, "to carry [the Lord's] name before Gentiles, kings, and Israelites" (9:15), a career change that will bring great suffering (v. 16). This commission comes to a temporarily blinded Saul through the mediation of a disciple named Ananias, who comes to the former enemy, lays hands on him, and assures him, "Brother Saul, the Lord sent me—Jesus, who appeared to you on the way as you were coming here. He sent me so that you could see again and be filled with the Holy Spirit" (v. 17). His physical (and spiritual) sight restored, Saul receives baptism (v. 18).

The Transformation of Saul (Paul): Takes One, Two, and Three

Acts narrates the story of Paul's dramatic turnaround from persecutor to preacher:

On the road to Damascus: 9:1-19

Twice more, the story is retold—with some variations—in the voice of the character Paul:

Just before his final arrest in Jerusalem: 22:3-21

In a defense speech before King Agrippa II and Festus, the governor of Judea: 26:9-18

Although there is no explicit mention of the realization of the divine purpose behind Ananias's visit—that Saul would be "filled with the Holy Spirit"—the rest of the story leaves little doubt. The bold, courageous preaching campaign this new recruit undertakes on behalf of the Lord Jesus bears the stamp of the Spirit. The mission gains a new voice, one that will eventually persuade Jews and Gentiles alike. With the Spirit in a supporting role here, God is in charge, even overcoming the menacing threat of an enemy like Saul.

Paul in Acts and in the Letters: A Study in Contrasts?

We meet Paul as a narrative character in Acts; in the letters we hear his own authorial voice. There are common themes, but the contrasts are impressive.

In both Acts and Paul's letters:

Paul begins as a fierce opponent of the early Christ followers before he becomes a vigorous advocate of their cause.

Paul's transformation is presented as the result of God's initiative.

Paul's mission involves frequent travel and occurs within Roman imperial space.

Paul's view of the Jewish law and his approach to inclusion of Gentiles are contested matters.

Paul self-identifies as a Jew whose commitment to the interpretation and practice of the Torah (law) was shaped by the tradition of the Pharisees.

Points of difference:

In Acts, Paul is said to be a Roman citizen from Tarsus who studied with Gamaliel and also bears the name Saul, a background the letters do not mention.

In Acts, the title of apostle is normally withheld from Paul (being limited instead to the Twelve, as in Acts 1:15-26, but see 14:14), while in the letters, Paul's authority is tied to his role as an apostle.

In Acts, Paul's activity primarily addresses Jewish audiences, while the letters present him as an "apostle to Gentiles."

In Acts, the emphasis is on the initial mission preaching of Paul, whose letter-writing goes unmentioned, while the letters center instead on Paul's ongoing nurture of the house churches he has formed and give little indication of Paul's initial mission talk.

In Acts, the mission speeches of Paul convey much the same message as Peter's: both deliver Luke's perspective; in the letters, we see Paul at work as a sophisticated thinker who brings his convictions about God to bear on the practical concerns of his churches.

The Holy Spirit plays an especially prominent part as mission director in the story of Peter's "conversion"—his radical shift in thinking—which results from his interaction with the Gentile soldier Cornelius (10:1-48). Detailed discussion of this passage will be delayed to the next section, but it is fitting to point out here that the fingerprints of the Spirit are evident throughout this episode. Peter comes to a radically new understanding of social and religious identity and of the boundaries of the movement: despite initial reluctance, he plays an instrumental role in extending the good-news message to non-Jews such as this Roman army officer and his household. The Holy Spirit ushers the premier apostle Simon Peter down a path he would not otherwise have taken. The result is the inclusion of Gentiles in the group.

A third, more mysterious passage shows the Holy Spirit as the character guiding the mission, this time of Paul:

> Paul and his companions traveled throughout the regions of Phrygia and Galatia *because the Holy Spirit kept them from speaking the word in the province of Asia.* When they approached the province of Mysia, they tried to enter the province of Bithynia, but *the Spirit of Jesus wouldn't let them.* Passing by Mysia, they went down to Troas instead. A vision of a man from Macedonia came to Paul during the night. He stood urging Paul, "Come over to Macedonia and help us!" Immediately after he saw the vision, we prepared to leave for the province of Macedonia, concluding that God had called us to proclaim the good news to them. (16:6-10; emphasis added)

As in other scenes in Acts (such as that featuring Cornelius), the activity of the Spirit and visionary experience merge to drive the plot and shape responses to events. Verse 10 is revealing: the leading of the Spirit and a dream-vision are not self-interpreting but require human discernment and decision. Paul concludes that through these signals God is directing him to take the good-news message to Macedonia rather than to linger in (the Roman province of) Asia or regions farther east in what is twenty-first-century Turkey. Luke spares readers the details, offering no hint about exactly how the Spirit hinders and thus redirects Paul's movement. This first appearance of the "we" character in Paul's company (also in 20:5-15; 21:1-18; 27:1–28:16) underscores the import of the geographic shift the Holy Spirit is effecting, whatever the specific details. What ensues is a period of vigorous mission activity by Paul and his associates in Philippi, Thessalonica, Athens, and Corinth, among other places (Acts 16–18). The Spirit leads the action; Paul diligently follows God's lead, and the Way moves onward toward the outer limits of the Roman Empire.

The Holy Spirit on the Frontier in Acts: Challenging Boundaries and Forming an Inclusive Community

History is full of surprises, but sometimes the sense of the unexpected is a matter of failure in memory and imagination. Luke's second volume tells of surprising twists and turns in the story of God's people, yet, it turns out, as events unfold they enact and fulfill ancient divine purposes. Leaders are guided by the divine Spirit to challenge and transgress conventional cultural boundaries and also to interpret those seemingly innovative moves in light of Israel's ancient scriptures. But those same leaders also resist what appears to be unwelcome change, a narrative pattern that makes clear that these moves to cross humanly constructed boundaries are the result of divine initiative, not human contrivance. The Holy Spirit plays a decisive role in these critical moments.

The Spirit fireworks on the day of Pentecost initiate this plot element. Spirit-infused Jesus followers are able to communicate their message in a way that speakers of various languages from many lands hear and comprehend (2:1-13). So the vision of a global mission encompassing many peoples, languages, and cultures begins to take shape. As Keener puts it, this gathering of representatives from all peoples "initiate[s] the church into the eschatological unity of an ethnically reconciled, cross-cultural people of God in the midst of the present age."[7]

Space Matters:
An Outline of the Narrative of Acts

1:1-11 Preface linking to the Gospel story; Preparation: Jesus's final instructions for his followers

1:12-26 More preparation: securing a full complement of twelve apostles

2:1–7:60 From Pentecost to persecution: **Mission in Jerusalem**

8:1-25 **Mission in Samaria**

8:26–28:31 **Mission to the End of the Earth** (Rome and Beyond)

***

Acts 1:8 credits this mission design to the final charge of Jesus and its execution to the empowerment of the Holy Spirit: "Rather, you will receive power when the Holy Spirit has come upon you; and you will be my witnesses in Jerusalem, in all Judea and Samaria, and to the end of the earth."

Although the mission at first is centered in Jerusalem and its environs in Judea, chapter 8 represents an important threshold, Samaria. Luke's Gospel has already highlighted the antagonism between Jews (from both Galilee and Judea) and Samaritans (Luke 9:52-55) but also the possibility of Samaritan fidelity to God (10:35-37; 17:11-19). Now, the itinerant evangelist Philip preaches the message of God's reign and of the Messiah Jesus, accompanying the message with dramatic acts of healing; this mission foray into Samaria leads many to believe and receive baptism (Acts

8:4-13). The apostles at Jerusalem send Peter and John to assess the situation (v. 14)—John, ironically, had responded with hostility when a Samaritan village rebuffed Jesus's disciples in Luke 9:52-55. Though the Samaritan converts have been baptized, a narrator's aside explains, the Holy Spirit has not come upon them (Acts 8:16). With prayer and the laying on of hands, they do receive the Spirit (vv. 15, 17). The Holy Spirit thus validates this extension of the message and authorizes the believing community to include Samaritan outsiders. The Spirit "prompts the apostles to recognize that they and the Samaritans [formerly outsiders to Peter and John's group] share…a common social identity."[8]

A humorous footnote to the story documents the failed attempt by the recently baptized Simon "the Great" to purchase the ability to control and convey the Spirit to people (vv. 18-24). Peter's harsh reply and Simon's remorse reinforce the point that the Holy Spirit and its gifts are not subject to human control. The apostles' teaching and the Spirit's arrival on the scene, however, do indicate what God's designs are: the Samaritans are welcome in the community of the Way.

But Philip extends the mission field even further—and so does the Spirit, too! In concert with an angel's message, the Spirit unexpectedly points Philip toward an encounter with an Ethiopian court official (8:26-39). This meeting with a God-worshipping African leader, who is eager to understand a passage he is reading from Isaiah, anticipates later developments that will indeed, beyond the narrative, usher the good news "to the end of the earth" (1:8; cf. 28:28). Framing the episode are mentions of the Spirit, who first directs Philip to approach the Ethiopian's chariot (v. 29) and then, Philip's work completed, whisks him to his next mission adventure (v. 39). The inclusive vision for the emerging movement to which God—through both angel and Spirit—is leading Philip welcomes a religiously serious African, and a eunuch at that. This is yet another indicator that all manner of persons are welcome in the people of God: this man's "lack of 'descendants' will not prohibit him from being incorporated into a new and large 'family.'"[9]

In the case of Samaria, Philip accepts the Samaritans, Peter and John endorse this development, and the Holy Spirit confirms their decision. An especially long episode in 10:1–11:18 places Peter in the forefront, though here he does not take the initiative but follows the lead of the Spirit in bringing the message about Jesus to Gentiles. This lengthy passage brings Peter the Galilean Jew to a Gentile household in Caesarea, to a Roman army officer named Cornelius (10:1-48). Then Peter returns to Jerusalem to account for his actions (11:1-18).

This episode highlights a Spirit-orchestrated challenge to ethnic boundaries. Cornelius's ethnic identity as a Roman is not erased, nor is Peter's as a Galilean Jew. But their encounter in the heart of the narrative signals God's purpose to create an inclusive community in which these particular ethnic identities do not separate but unite, though without erasing the difference between them. There are other markers of divine initiative (dream-visions, heavenly messengers) here, but it is noteworthy that this pivotal episode of Acts that is "most concerned with ethnic boundaries is also the section containing the densest cluster of Spirit-references," eight in all.[10]

Soldiers sent by the Roman army officer inquire after Simon-named-Peter, even as he is puzzled about the meaning of his threefold vision urging him to eat "unclean" animals. The Spirit removes any ambiguity, directing Peter to accompany the men without question (10:19-20). At Cornelius's home, the apostle finally connects the dots of divine tutelage, recognizing that God's impartiality means that people of every group and nation are accepted by God (vv. 34-35). He proceeds to deliver an elegant summary of the Lukan Gospel's presentation of Jesus, the Messiah and universal Lord (vv. 36-41). Verse 38 highlights God's Spirit-anointing of Jesus (echoing Luke 3:21-22; 4:1-15) as empowerment for his ministry of healing and liberation. The speech then shifts to the apostles' role as witnesses who attest that God has appointed Jesus to be not only judge of all people but also the one through whom all who believe receive forgiveness (Acts 10:42-43).

Peter has made all his key points, so nothing is lacking when his speech is interrupted (a literary device of which Luke is fond).[11] In dramatic fashion, the Holy Spirit seals the deal, with a Pentecost-like interruption confirming that the gospel message Peter has presented belongs also to Gentiles:

> While Peter was still speaking, the Holy Spirit fell on everyone who heard the word. The circumcised believers who had come with Peter were astonished that the gift of the Holy Spirit had been poured out even on the Gentiles. They heard them speaking in other languages and praising God. Peter asked, "These people have received the Holy Spirit just as we have. Surely no one can stop them from being baptized with water, can they?" (10:44-47)

The sequence of events is surprising. Before any mention of a believing response, and before any suggestion of baptism, the Holy Spirit falls upon these Gentiles in a Roman army officer's household. This exceptional pattern leaves no doubt: God has said yes to these people, so who would prevent their being welcomed through the incorporation ritual of baptism? The Spirit is thus leading the community to challenge and transgress conventional social boundaries and welcome Gentile outsiders into the people of God.

Twice in the ensuing narrative, Peter will defend his actions, pointing through them to the Spirit's initiative (11:1-18; 15:7-11). The first time, his report convinces skeptics in Jerusalem: "Once the apostles and other believers heard this, they calmed down. They praised God and concluded, 'So then God has enabled Gentiles to change their hearts and lives so that they might have new life'" (11:18). The second time, in the very center of Acts, Peter's testimony is joined by that of Paul and Barnabas, who report "what God had accomplished" among the Gentiles through their work (15:2-5 [v. 4]). James, the brother of Jesus, by now a chief leader in the Jerusalem group, adds the confirming witness of scripture (15:16-18, quoting from Amos 9:11-12):

> "After this I will return, and I will rebuild David's fallen tent; I will rebuild what has been torn down. I will restore it so that the rest of humanity will seek the Lord, even all the Gentiles who belong to me." The Lord says this, the one who does these things known from earliest times. (Acts 15:16-18)

Scripture and Spirit-guided experience join hands to draw Gentiles into the people of God, and James interprets this development not as a disconcerting innovation but as the realization of God's long-standing design for Israel.

In the various aspects of the development of the Holy Spirit as an active character in Luke-Acts, what we are glimpsing is the activity of God. As William Shepherd has emphasized, the Holy Spirit delivers and seals the reliability in story-telling that Luke's preface placed in the foreground of the author's concerns (Luke 1:4): "The character of the Holy Spirit signals narrative reliability, and . . . ultimately the Spirit's presence and action is that of God. . . . What is at stake for Luke in his portrayal of the Spirit—and indeed his entire narrative—is the very reliability of God."[12] The Holy Spirit helps Luke's audience gain confidence that the grand story he is telling is the story of God's activity for the sake of God's people Israel—and for the sake of all peoples of the earth.

All Wet, but No Spirit: A Puzzling Episode (Acts 19:1-7)

One fascinating episode still awaits discussion. By the time readers come to a scene set in Ephesus in chapter 19, they are well acquainted with the links among believing response to the message, baptism, and experience of the Holy Spirit—sometimes manifested in tongues speech, sometimes not. The pattern has exhibited variations, however, that pique audience interest. For example, in Samaria, acceptance of Philip's message and baptism precede experience of the Spirit, which is delayed until Peter and John have arrived from Jerusalem (8:12-17). By contrast, in the Cornelius story, the Spirit jumps in ahead of believing response to Peter's message, and baptism then follows as a confirming ritual (10:44-48). Such variations suggest that Luke's narrative does not commend a single pattern of conversion and initiation (e.g., preaching of the message → believing response → baptism → experience/gifts of the Spirit). These events vary in sequence from episode to episode, and signs of the Spirit (notably, speaking in tongues) are not always evident. The delayed appearance of the Spirit in Samaria and its early arrival at the house of Cornelius draw readers' attention to the pivotal and momentous scenes being played out in Samaria and in the Roman army officer's home. The narrative does not define one or another paradigm for an individual's conversion, experience of the Spirit, and incorporation in the community.[13] Rather, Luke is telling the story of the restoration and expansion of the people of God, encompassing all nations, in the decisive era of end-time fulfillment that *is* the age of the Spirit (notice the phrase "last days" in Acts 2:17, Luke's addition to the passage quoted from Joel 2:28-32 = LXX 3:1-5).

Prophetic Spirit in the Last Days: Joel and Acts

Joel 2:28

After that I will pour out my spirit upon everyone;

your sons and your daughters will prophesy,

your old men will dream dreams,

and your young men will see visions.

Acts 2:17

In the last days, God says,

I will pour out my Spirit on all people.

Your sons and daughters will prophesy.

Your young will see visions.

Your elders will dream dreams.

When readers reach Acts 19, then, they do not have reason to conceive of faith, baptism, and experience of the Spirit as conforming to a single, consistent pattern of narration. Still, the passage is surprising and puzzling. In 18:24-28, Priscilla and Aquila help the articulate Alexandrian Jew Apollos gain a more accurate understanding of the beliefs and practices of the Way. He had only been aware of—or, perhaps, experienced—the baptism of John (v. 25). There is no mention of the Spirit in this obscure passage, but is the implication that Apollos had not received the fuller baptism that includes experience of the Holy Spirit? The unit that follows suggests as much.

> While Apollos was in Corinth, Paul took a route through the interior and came to Ephesus, where he found some disciples. He asked them, "Did you receive the Holy Spirit when you came to believe?" They replied, "We've not even heard that there is a Holy Spirit." Then he said, "What baptism did you receive, then?" They answered, "John's baptism." Paul explained, "John baptized with a baptism by which people showed they were changing their hearts and lives. It was a baptism that told people about the one who was coming after him. This is the one in whom they were to believe. This one is Jesus." After they listened to Paul, they were baptized in the name of the Lord Jesus. When Paul placed his hands on them, the Holy Spirit came on them, and they began speaking in other languages and prophesying. Altogether, there were about twelve people. (19:1-7)

A baptism centering on repentance—John's ritual—is not enough. It is after baptism "in the name of the Lord Jesus" (v. 5), coupled with the laying on of hands, that the gifts of the Holy Spirit (here, speech in tongues and prophecy) come to the believer. Moreover, when viewed in the grand sweep of Luke's narrative, the problem for these twelve is that they are still waiting for a reality—the gift of God's Spirit in the messianic era—that has already been fulfilled.[14]

The story told in Acts 19:1-7 has often been taken, especially in Pentecostal circles, to point to the normative pattern for individuals' experience of conversion and initiation into the Christian community. Confession of faith precedes baptism (in the name of Jesus or the triune God as in Matt 28:19), and then endowment with the Spirit, manifested in speaking in tongues, ensues. This pattern has already been narrated in Acts 2:37-39, though the actual experience of the Spirit for those first converts is not reported. Yet debate about this view has become spirited within Pentecostal traditions and in dialogue between them and other Christian interpreters.

It is helpful, in evaluating these debates, to focus on the rhetorical interests of the story as Luke has told it, and to refrain from imposing on the narrative a doctrinal system constructed to serve later interests. Both 8:14-17 and 19:1-7 present exceptional cases where there is a disconnect between initial preaching, believing response, and baptism, on the one hand, and the reception of the Holy Spirit, on the other. In the first case, the boundary-crossing move to include the Samaritans requires dual validation by both the Jerusalem-based apostles and the Spirit: this is God's initiative and design! However, there is no explicit mention of speaking in tongues as the marker of the Spirit's presence, such as occurs in both 10:44-46 and 19:6. In the second case (19:1-7), it is Paul who completes and validates the conversion of the circle associated with Apollos; this is a move to legitimate Paul above the leadership of Apollos—and of the Way above a continuing, rival movement centered on John the Baptizer. Verse 6 highlights the evidence for the Spirit's presence with the phenomena of speaking in tongues and prophecy. Underlying the legitimation of Paul, therefore, is once again the initiative of God. The unusual pattern of Spirit and faith/baptism in each case thus serves particular rhetorical concerns related to those episodes in the narrative.

Summary

Even before Jesus steps onto the world stage, Luke prepares for his arrival with a burst of Spirit-inspired prophetic speech celebrating the fulfillment of ancient promises of salvation for God's people (Spirit-prompted Zechariah and Simeon in Luke 1–2). Fast-forward to the thirty-year-old Jesus about to undertake his mission: in chapters 3 and 4 Luke could not paint in bolder colors the Spirit's dynamic presence. Jesus receives baptism attended by a Spirit-dove, undergoes strenuous vocational testing accompanied by the Spirit, and then—full of Spirit-power—begins his prophetic ministry of teaching, healing, and liberating the oppressed. Although the Spirit scarcely figures in the rest of the Gospel narrative, Luke has scored the point memorably: Jesus speaks and acts as one empowered by the divine Spirit, one in whom God's gracious and liberating presence is met.

After his death and resurrection, Jesus tasks his followers, led by the twelve apostle-witnesses, to continue his mission, but now to extend it to the farthest reaches of the world. Only when the Holy Spirit descends at Pentecost, however, are the disciples equipped for that daunting task (Acts 2). Power from on high, from God, Jesus imparts to them (2:33; Luke 24:49), and the result is swift and dramatic. Peter speaks boldly and persuasively, and a movement—a Way to the end of the earth—is launched. The Holy Spirit continues to play an active part as the drama unfolds, informing prophetic speech, directing the course of the mission, and especially pressing the apostles to transgress conventional boundaries of culture, ethnicity, and religion. If Samaritans (Acts 8) and then Gentiles (Acts 10) join the movement, it is not because of the innovativeness of followers like Philip or Peter but because of the initiative and prodding of the Holy Spirit. So God begins to fashion a multicultural, multiethnic, world-encompassing movement. With urgency born of the belief that history's last chapter has dawned (in Peter's recall of the prophecy of Joel 2:28-32 in Acts 2:17-21), young and old, male and female, Jew and Gentile (Samaritan, too), slave and free will dare to imagine—and boldly proclaim—a world that conforms to the character not of the Roman Empire but of a new sovereign, the Messiah Jesus. On a stage that Rome dominates, it will take a generous outpouring of the Holy Spirit to equip the apostolic band for their mission. And that is exactly how Luke tells the story.

For Further Reading

Carroll, John T. *Jesus and the Gospels: An Introduction*. Louisville: Westminster John Knox, 2016.

Gaventa, Beverly Roberts. *The Acts of the Apostles*. ANTC. Nashville: Abingdon, 2003.

Hur, Ju. *A Dynamic Reading of the Holy Spirit in Luke-Acts*. JSNTSup 211. Sheffield: Sheffield Academic, 2001.

Johnson, Luke Timothy. *The Acts of the Apostles*. SP 5. Collegeville, MN: Liturgical Press, 1992.

Keener, Craig S. *Acts: An Exegetical Commentary*. 4 vols. Grand Rapids: Baker, 2012–2015.

———. *The Spirit in the Gospels and Acts: Divine Purity and Power*. Peabody, MA: Hendrickson, 1997. Repr., Grand Rapids: Baker, 2010.

Kuecker, Aaron J. *Spirit and the "Other": Social Identity, Ethnicity and Intergroup Reconciliation in Luke-Acts*. LNTS 444. London: T and T Clark, 2011.

Levison, John R. *Filled with the Spirit*. Grand Rapids: Eerdmans, 2009.

———. *Inspired: The Holy Spirit and the Mind of Faith*. Grand Rapids: Eerdmans, 2013.

Peppard, Michael. *The Son of God in the Roman World: Divine Sonship in Its Social and Political Context*. New York: Oxford University Press, 2011.

Schweizer, Eduard. *The Holy Spirit*. Translated by Reginald H. Fuller and Ilse Fuller. Philadelphia: Fortress, 1980.

Shepherd, William H. *The Narrative Function of the Holy Spirit as a Character in Luke-Acts*. SBLDS 147. Atlanta: Scholars Press, 1994.

Smith, Daniel Lynwood. *The Rhetoric of Interruption: Speech-Making, Turn-Taking, and Rule-Breaking in Luke-Acts and Ancient Greek Narrative*. BZNW 193. Berlin: de Gruyter, 2012.

Turner, Max. *Power from on High: The Spirit in Israel's Restoration and Witness in Luke-Acts*. JPTSup 9. Sheffield: Sheffield Academic Press, 1996. Repr., Eugene, OR: Wipf and Stock, 2015.

Wenk, Matthias. "Acts." Pages 116–28 in *A Biblical Theology of the Holy Spirit*. Edited by Trevor J. Burke and Keith Warrington. Eugene, OR: Cascade, 2014.

———. *Community-Forming Power: The Socio-Ethical Role of the Spirit in Luke-Acts*. JPTSup 19. Sheffield: Sheffield Academic Press, 2000.

Chapter 6

The Spirit-Paraclete in the Gospel of John and First John

As in so many other ways, the Gospel of John offers a distinctive perspective on the Spirit, one that differs in intriguing ways from the Synoptic Gospels (Matthew, Mark, and Luke).[1] The most remarkable feature of John's treatment of the Holy Spirit is the image of the Paraclete. Jesus's farewell speeches to his disciples in John 13–17 employ this image to bring into sharp focus the role and activity of the Spirit. *Paraclete* is a transliteration of the Greek word *paraklētos*, which can mean *advocate*, *helper*, *comforter*. As Paraclete, the Spirit continues the work of Jesus after his departure (i.e., after Easter), revealing the character and life-imparting activity of God and tutoring Jesus's followers to remember, interpret, and communicate his words and acts—an abiding, consoling presence with the disciples and a vigorous witness to truth before an often hostile world.

Jesus and Spirit in John 1–12

Chapters 1–12 narrate the public activity of Jesus, featuring lengthy speeches and dialogues—often in the form of vigorous debates—and a set of seven extraordinary actions by Jesus, which John calls "signs." These actions, with the interpreting commentary Jesus provides, point to his identity and significance. The ministry of Jesus in John's Gospel is centered in

Jerusalem and Judea, and his words and acts spark intense conflict over the claims he makes for his role as the revealer sent by God, as God's agent who uniquely carries divine authority to give life to those who believe him and to pronounce judgment on refusal to believe.

Seven Signs by Jesus Narrated in John's Gospel

Wedding at Cana: water turned into wine (2:1-11)

Healing of a royal official's son (4:46-54)

Healing for a paralyzed man on the Sabbath (5:1-9)

Feeding of a large crowd (6:1-14)

Walking upon the lake (6:16-21; though without explicit mention of a sign)

Giving sight to a man born with blindness (9:1-7)

Restoring life to dead Lazarus (11:1-47)

As in the other Gospels, the baptism of Jesus by John is a Spirit-anointing that conveys his identity as beloved Son of God and prepares him for his mission. In John's narrative, however, significance lies less in the ritual of baptismal washing than in the public witness to Jesus that the baptizing prophet declares: Jesus is the Son of God and the Lamb of God who removes the world's sin (1:29-34). Of particular interest here is John's testimony that Jesus will baptize with the Holy Spirit precisely as the one upon whom the Spirit descends and *remains*: "The one on whom you see the Spirit coming down and resting is the one who baptizes with the Holy Spirit" (1:33). From the outset, the narrative forges an intimate relation between Jesus the Son of God and the Holy Spirit. At story's end, he will impart to others the very Spirit that animates his mission (20:22).

A night-time conversation between Jesus and the prominent Pharisee-teacher Nicodemus accents the sovereign freedom of the Spirit and its key role in the shift in perception and understanding that John calls "believing" (3:1-10). The narration plays with dual meanings of both *pneuma* (wind, spirit) and the Greek adverb *anōthen* (again, from above). Jesus tells Nicodemus that only those who are born *anōthen* can see God's realm (3:3). Nicodemus focuses on only one of these meanings—"again"—and so is baffled by the notion that he needs to reenter his mother's womb for a second birth. But Jesus pictures this rebirth as one "with water and the Spirit" (vv. 4-5)—that is, from above, from God. He then contrasts two domains in which one may be born: flesh and spirit (v. 6). Physical birth into a world that God created but that does not know God is not enough. True understanding must come in a spiritual enlightenment that has its source in God and comes through the Spirit. But who and how? This is a matter humans do not control: "God's Spirit [or wind: *pneuma*] blows wherever it wishes. You hear its sound, but you don't know where it comes from or where it is going. It's the same with everyone who is born of the Spirit [*pneumatos*]" (v. 8). In John's narrative world, only people who are responsive to the deep truth about God that Jesus speaks—as the one who comes from God/above, the one in whom the Spirit "remains" (is continually present)—"get it" and can experience the fullness of life that God intends and that believing humans receive. At this point in the story, it is unclear if Nicodemus will become one of those who do believe, who are "born of the Spirit," born from above. For now, he does not understand; later, though, his public gesture of honoring Jesus in burial is a promising indicator (19:38-42).

John 4 presents Jesus with another partner in theological debate, this time a Samaritan woman. Though doubly marginalized in first-century Judean culture as a woman and a Samaritan outsider, the woman more than holds her own in a serious theological discussion with Jesus. After talking about water drawn from a well, in contrast to the "living water" that Jesus can supply (vv. 10-15), and about the woman's history of multiple marriages (vv. 16-19), the two consider the competing claims by Samaritans and Jews to the location of the temple where God's holy presence truly resides (4:19-24). Because "God is spirit," Jesus maintains, divine presence and worship of God transcend any physical temple site (cf. 2:19-21), and those who worship God "must worship in spirit and truth" (vv. 23-24). The "the time is coming—and is here!" when this will occur. By the end of the Gospel, when Jesus has been lifted up—on a cross, yet in glory—the time for authentic worship of God who is Spirit will have arrived, though already in Jesus's presence, as the Spirit-bearer, this can happen. The Samaritan woman proceeds to illustrate that this is so, as she accepts Jesus's claim to be the Messiah and draws her whole village toward exuberant acclamation of him as "Savior of the world" (vv. 25-42).

The affirmation that "God is spirit" pictures God "as other than flesh, mortal, and confined in space and time" (e.g., in a temple, whether in Jerusalem or on Mount Gerizim in Samaria).[2] In this passage, which relates a successful mission among Samaritan outsiders, anticipating later initiatives in mission (cf. Acts 8), John depicts the Spirit of God as a "life-giving force through which God calls a new people into being."[3] This presentation differs greatly from the Synoptic Gospels' depiction of the Spirit as the power that fuels Jesus's acts of healing and liberates persons from oppression by unclean spirits (see chs. 4 and 5 above).

The well scene of chapter 4 juxtaposes the images of water and Spirit, yet it is not until a set of debates in Jerusalem on the occasion of the Feast of Tabernacles (7:2) that John explicitly connects water and spirit:

> On the last and most important day of the festival, Jesus stood up and shouted, "All who are thirsty should come to me! All who believe in me should drink! As the scriptures said concerning me, 'Rivers of living water will flow out from within him.'" Jesus said this concerning the Spirit. Those who believed in him would soon receive the Spirit, but they hadn't experienced the Spirit yet since Jesus hadn't yet been glorified. (7:37-39)

The spatial-temporal setting is significant. In Jesus's assertion, the evocative symbolism of Spirit as life-giving water shifts from the temple to Jesus and from the Feast of Tabernacles to any time the Spirit is present.

This is an obscure passage in at least two ways. A first puzzle arises from the narrator's statement that "there was no Spirit" prior to Jesus's departure in glory. How do readers make sense of this assertion in view of the Spirit's presence earlier in the narrative (esp. 1:33)? In one sense, the Spirit is already present and active in Jesus's words and acts. But not until after he has been elevated on a cross and thus glorified by God will Jesus impart the Spirit to his followers. With his dying breath on the cross, Jesus "hands over" the *pneuma*—his spirit-breath (19:30)—and at a soldier's spear thrust, water with blood flows from his lifeless body (19:34). On Easter evening he breathes on the disciples, and accompanying his breath are words that effect the reality they name: "Receive the Holy Spirit" (20:22). After Jesus has returned to the Father (God), the Paraclete-Spirit will be present among Jesus's disciples and equip them to continue his mission in the world. He will re-present Jesus to them, and through their witness, to the world.

A second puzzle is this: there is ambiguity in reference and punctuation. Although the NRSV pictures "rivers of living water" flowing from the heart (literally, belly) of the believer, an alternative translation of verses 38-39 might be: "If anyone is thirsty, let him come to me, and let the one who believes in me drink. As the scripture has said, 'Streams of living water will flow from within him [i.e., Jesus].'"[4] Is Jesus or the believer the source of flowing water? The sharp christological focus of this Gospel (e.g., the frequent "I am" declarations) suggests that, as in the conversation at the well of Jacob (in 4:14), *Jesus* is the source of living water—or, in the symbolism of these verses, the one from whom the Spirit will issue. Indeed, with a shift in images from water (drinking) to air (breathing), Jesus will later enact this promise (20:22). Jesus, not believers, possesses divine authority to bestow Spirit-life. Yet the ambiguity of reference permits John's readers to read backward from the end of the story. Here they may discover a hint that while during his public activity Jesus (by conferral from the Father) is the source of life-giving water/Spirit, after his departure the disciples will be Spirit-empowered to mediate this offer of life abundant whenever they give their Paraclete-tutored witness to the world. In either case, the imagery of 7:37-39—rivers of rushing, living water—suggests lavish abundance in this divine gift of life for humankind. This "magnificent river from within will bring life: life to the fullest, life without measure."[5]

Jesus's "I Am" Sayings in John's Gospel

bread of life (or from heaven)

light of the world

gate for the sheep

good shepherd

resurrection and the life

the way, the truth, the life

vine

The Spirit-Paraclete of the Farewell Speeches

With the approach of Passover (the third one mentioned in John's account of the public career of Jesus), Jesus withdraws from his conflict-riddled public engagements (ch. 12). In chapters 13–17, he shares a private meal with his closest friends, the disciples. In that setting he prepares them for what lies ahead, not least his betrayal by Judas, his arrest, his death, and their life afterward. At the meal, Jesus employs a foot-washing ritual to model the other-serving humility he commends for his followers (13:1-20). Beginning with the foot-washing, an expansive farewell discourse-with-dialogue spanning four chapters culminates in a poignant prayer in which Jesus pleads for the disciples' unity, patterned after the unity he enjoys with the Father who sent him (13:1–17:26). Within this farewell scene, four passages highlight the role and activity of the Holy Spirit, consistently labeled the Paraclete by Jesus (14:15-18, 25-28; 15:26-27; 16:7-15).

Spirit-Paraclete	Role/activity	Jesus
14:16, 26	given, sent by the Father	3:16; 5:30, 36-38; 8:16, 18; 12:49; 17:18, 25; etc.
15:26; 16:7, 13	comes into the world	5:43; 16:28; 18:37
14:17	not accepted by the world	1:11; 5:43
14:17	not known by the world	8:19; 16:3
14:26	teaches	7:14-17; 18:19-20
15:26	testifies/gives witness	5:31-47; 7:7; 8:13-18; 18:37
16:13	speaks what he has heard, not on own	8:26; 14:10
16:13; cf. 14:17; 15:26	guides into all truth "Spirit of truth"	14:6; 18:37
16:14	honors the one who sent him	12:28; 17:1, 4
14:16, 26; etc.	is Paraclete/Advocate	14:16; 1 John 2:1

In John 14–16, the Spirit-Paraclete is a teacher "who reminds the disciples of Jesus' words (14:26), testifies on Jesus' behalf (15:26), glorifies Jesus (16:14), and accuses or convicts the world of sin (16:7-8)."[6] Aptly, within the setting of this farewell scene, Jesus accents the pivotal role the Holy Spirit will play in bridging the time of Jesus's physical presence among the disciples to the future beyond Easter when he will not be with them. Though absent, he will not leave them orphaned and abandoned (14:16, 18): the Spirit will continually re-present him as the agent of divine presence.

Jesus and the Spirit: Parallel Paracletes

The profiles John sketches for Jesus and the Spirit-Paraclete show many parallels; the Paraclete is a successor to Jesus and, after his departure, does what he had done.[7] Like Jesus, the Spirit comes from God (15:26; 16:7,

13), is sent by God (14:26; 15:26; 16:7), and is welcomed and known by believers (14:16-17). The "overlapping functions of Jesus and the Spirit" primarily have to do with teaching and revealing the word of God (by speaking of what they have heard) and with giving testimony.[8]

As Thompson has emphasized, however, the Spirit-Paraclete also shares many traits and activities with God:

- testifying to Jesus (5:37; 8:18 ➔ 15:26-27)[9]

- honoring/glorifying Jesus (5:44; 8:54; 13:31-32; 17:1, 5 ➔ 16:14)

- being with the disciples (14:23; 17:11, 15, 26 ➔ 14:17)

- having authority to judge/convict (5:22, 27, 30; 8:16 ➔ 16:8-11)

- teaching (7:16-17; cf. 1 John 2:26-27 ➔ 14:26; 16:13)

So, as a successor to Jesus in the role of teacher and revealer, the Spirit-Paraclete also carries on the work of God (the Father).[10]

At the same time, in the situation of John's author and audience (and thereafter), the world that encounters the community of disciples will experience the Spirit-Paraclete in and through the testimony that Jesus's followers give in speech and action: "If Jesus is the Word embodied as a human being, then the Paraclete is the Spirit 'embodied' in, among, and through the community of disciples (14:16)."[11] The witness given by followers of Jesus will meet a hostile response just as Jesus's did (e.g., 17:14-16, 25). Because the Paraclete as "Spirit of truth" (14:27; 15:26; 16:13) confronts the world with the truth through the medium of the disciples' speech, one dimension of the Spirit-Paraclete's activity will be as prosecuting attorney:

> When the Companion [or Advocate] comes, whom I will send from the Father—the Spirit of Truth who proceeds from the Father—he will testify about me. You will testify too, because you have been with me from the beginning. (15:26-27)

> When he comes, he will show the world it was wrong about sin, righteousness, and judgment. He will show the world it was wrong about sin because they don't believe in me. He will show the world it was wrong about righteousness because I'm going to the Father and you won't see me anymore. He will show the world it was wrong about judgment because this world's ruler stands condemned. (16:8-11)

The signature "takes" in John's Gospel on the weighty notions of sin, righteousness (or justice: *dikaiosynē* in Greek), and judgment are very much in evidence here. As in Jesus's own mission in chapters 1–12, "sin" means primarily a failure to believe in Jesus as the one who makes God known. "Righteousness," right relation to God, continues to be oriented around Jesus as the one sent from the Father to do this revealing, even after Jesus's lifetime. And "judgment" has already been pronounced over the powers that hold sway in this world and oppose the work of God (in John's world, these powers are the Roman Empire). This "truth" about the world and its true character the disciples will speak audaciously, and when they do, their voices will convey the witness of the Spirit-Paraclete as prosecutor. In this cosmic trial—extending into the future the "trial" of Jesus that has unfolded throughout his public activity[12]—the Spirit plays the role of advocate who stands with the disciples and also of prosecutor who accuses the world of commitment to a way that subverts truth and right. When their message receives a favorable response, though, the Spirit will be experienced as life-giving and restorative.

This presence and activity of the Spirit-Paraclete in the witness of the disciples finds symbolic representation in the narrative in the anonymous character of the beloved disciple. The future tasks that Jesus predicts for the Paraclete correspond in important ways to the role the beloved disciple will play, guiding the community, giving testimony to Jesus, and calling to memory the teaching of Jesus (e.g., 21:24).[13]

The Spirit-Paraclete has the role of teacher, guiding Jesus's followers, leading them to grasp all truth. The fund of knowledge available to them will grow, to be sure, but what counts as genuine knowledge or wisdom and what is foolish contrivance will be a matter of debate, as the letters of John amply document. Claims to be teaching under the direction and inspiration of the Spirit were sometimes vigorously contested (1 John 4:1-6; cf. 2:19, 22, 26-27; 2 John 7, 9-11). According to the Gospel of John, the knowledge to which the Paraclete will open up access will be recognizable because it coheres with the core message of Jesus, which it is the primary task of the Spirit to call to memory.

> The Companion [or Advocate], the Holy Spirit, whom the Father will send in my name, will teach you everything and will remind you of everything I told you. (14:26)

> However, when the Spirit of Truth comes, he will guide you in all truth. He won't speak on his own, but will say whatever he hears and will proclaim to you what is to come. He will glorify me, because he will take what is mine and proclaim it to you. Everything that the Father has is mine. That's why I said that the Spirit takes what is mine and will proclaim it to you. (16:13-15)

Especially important, and a welcome accent in this farewell scene, the Spirit-Paraclete will be the Advocate in the form of a consoling, encouraging presence within and among the community of disciples after Jesus's post-Easter departure. The Spirit-Paraclete will remain with them; they will not be left alone and unsupported: "I will ask the Father, and he will send another [Advocate], who will be with you forever. This [Advocate] is the Spirit of Truth.... You know him, because he lives with you and will be with you" (14:16-17). Though no longer in Jesus's physical company, the disciples will continue to experience divine presence (of both Father and Son) in the form of the Spirit-Paraclete. A sorrowful farewell scene thus also joyfully anticipates a new mode of intimate connection between human and divine.

Spirit-breath: From Jesus to the Mission of the Disciples (John 19–20)

In a way that suits the christological focus of this Gospel, Jesus himself effects this transition. He hands over his spirit with his dying breath (19:30) and then, on Easter, breathes on his closest friends, speaking words that convey the gift of the Spirit:

> Jesus said to them again, "Peace be with you. As the Father sent me, so I am sending you." Then he breathed on them and said, "Receive the Holy Spirit. If you forgive anyone's sins, they are forgiven; if you don't forgive them, they aren't forgiven." (20:21-23)

It is under the guidance and empowerment of the Holy Spirit that the disciples will be Jesus's agents, extending his mission in the world and authorized to discern and judge well (retaining or forgiving sins). Only those well tutored and guided by the Spirit-Paraclete dare undertake that responsibility.

Spirit Transformations in the First Letter of John

After the composition of the Gospel of John, life went on in the earliest communities of its readers. As it turns out, the poignant petition for the disciples' unity that looms so large in the prayer of John 17 amounted to an uncanny reading of the handwriting on the wall. The three short letters called First, Second, and Third John indicate that conflict within these groups of Jesus followers became intense and eventually led to schism.[14] While conflict evidently centered on differing understandings of the identity and role of Jesus (i.e., Christology; see, e.g., 1 John 2:22-23; 4:1-3; 2 John 7, 9-11), this tense situation also generated a new way of viewing the work of the Holy Spirit. The Spirit remains prominent in 1 John but has a new look. Notably, there is only one reference to the Paraclete in the Letters of John, and it points not to the Holy Spirit but instead to Jesus: "We have an advocate with the Father, Jesus Christ the righteous one. He is God's way of dealing with our sins, not only ours but the sins of the whole world" (1 John 2:1-2). It is likely that the disconnect between Paraclete and Spirit in the Johannine letters is the result of theological innovations disconcerting to the author of 1 John, ideas that the group with which he is in conflict attribute to the instruction of the Spirit-Paraclete.[15] (The late second-century Montanist group would later make precisely this sort of appeal to the Paraclete of John's Gospel as warrant for its innovative teachings about Christian faith.)

Montanists and John's Paraclete

Montanus flourished late second century CE, and the movement he launched recruited followers for several centuries

Montanists appealed to the Paraclete as source of their inspired "new prophecy"

Women such as Prisca and Maximilla were among the Paraclete-inspired prophets

They located the New Jerusalem of Revelation 20–21 in Phrygia (western Asia Minor)

They advocated a rigorous ethic and ascetic lifestyle

The emerging "great church" rejected the Montanist teaching and its appropriation of John's Gospel and its Paraclete image

In other ways, too, 1 John offers a distinctive perspective on the Spirit. Like the Gospel of John, this letter is marked by sharp polarity and division, but the opposition between the truth Jesus and his Paraclete-guided disciples impart and a world that so often resists it now morphs into a conflict within the believing community between two spirits, the s/Spirit of truth and a spirit of deceit or error. Naturally, the author identifies his own teaching with the former and the views of his (also Christ believing) opponents with the latter.[16] This sharp divide between spirits of truth and error is similar to what we find in a number of late Second-Temple Jewish writings, including the Testament of Judah (20:1) and the Dead Sea Scrolls (e.g., in the *Rule of the Community*, 1QS III, 17-19; IV, 2-14).[17] The author of 1 John speaks from a posture of authority, confident that his teaching carries the imprimatur of the truth while his adversaries have turned away from truth and are now beyond the community's boundaries (see 2 John 7, 9-11). The sovereign freedom of the Spirit to move where and in whom it wishes (John 3:8) seems to be much constrained by the leadership of the letter's author and his teaching circle.

94

In light of the emphasis in 1 John on competing spirits of truth and error at work in the community, it is unsurprising that the letter summons readers to "test the spirits" so as to discern whether prophetic teaching is to be trusted. Not every claim to be speaking with the authorization of the divine Spirit is legitimate. Some speak as "false prophets"—indeed, their message is inspired by the "spirit of antichrist" (1 John 4:3; cf. 2:22; 2 John 7)!

> Dear friends, don't believe every spirit. Test the spirits to see if they are from God because many false prophets have gone into the world. This is how you know if a spirit comes from God: every spirit that confesses that Jesus Christ has come as a human is from God, and every spirit that doesn't confess Jesus is not from God. This is the spirit of the antichrist, which you have heard is coming and is now already in the world.... We are from God. The person who knows God listens to us. Whoever is not from God doesn't listen to us. This is how we recognize the Spirit of truth and the spirit of error. (1 John 4:1-6)

Faithful adherence to the genuine Christology of the author and his circle is the criterion by which it is apparent which spirit (truth or error) animates one's convictions.[18] And in this sense the author and his allies are confident that they are gifted with Spirit-presence and so "remain in [God] and he remains in us" (4:13). The image of the Spirit in 1 John reflects the heated polemics in which the letter arose.

The other test the letter offers of participation in the Spirit is twofold: obedience to the primary commandment to believe in Jesus the Son of God (specifically as fully human, including a real suffering and crucifixion-death) and the not-so "new commandment" of love for one another (3:23-24). The letter holds together theological and ethical strands (belief and ethical practice) that clearly stood in tension within the community of the letter's earliest readers.

A final distinctive accent in 1 John is the theme of witness-to-truth, so prominent in John's Gospel and also present in the letter—but with a difference. In an obscure passage, the author relates the theme of testimony/witness to the linked images of water and blood, as the Gospel's crucifixion scene also does (John 19:34-35). Now the Spirit—embodying truth—is cast in the role of testifying witness, and it appears that the Spirit's key testimony (whatever the elusive meaning of some of the details) is to the authentic, full humanity of Jesus in birth (water) and death (blood). Thus the Spirit of truth appropriates the imagery of water and blood to press home a right understanding of the identity of the Son of God (1 John 5:6-8). This is the witness about which the letter seeks to convince its hearers.

For Further Reading

Bennema, Cornelis. "The Giving of the Spirit in John 19–20: Another Round." Pages 86–104 in *The Spirit and Christ in the New Testament and Christian Theology: Essays in Honor of Max Turner*. Edited by I. Howard Marshall, Volker Rabens, and Cornelis Bennema. Grand Rapids: Eerdmans, 2012.

———. *The Power of Saving Wisdom*. WUNT 2/148. Tübingen: Mohr Siebeck, 2002.

Boring, M. Eugene. *An Introduction to the New Testament: History, Literature, Theology*. Louisville: Westminster John Knox, 2012.

Brown, Tricia Gates. *Spirit in the Writings of John: Johannine Pneumatology in Social-Scientific Perspective*. JSNTSup 253. London: T and T Clark International, 2003.

Burge, Gary M. *The Anointed Community: The Holy Spirit in the Johannine Tradition*. Grand Rapids: Eerdmans, 1987.

———. "The Gospel of John." Pages 104–15 in *A Biblical Theology of the Holy Spirit*. Edited by Trevor J. Burke and Keith Warrington. Eugene, OR: Cascade, 2014.

Carroll, John T. *Jesus and the Gospels: An Introduction*. Louisville: Westminster John Knox, 2016.

Culpepper, R. Alan. *The Gospel and Letters of John*. IBT. Nashville: Abingdon, 1998.

Koester, Craig R. *The Word of Life: A Theology of John's Gospel*. Grand Rapids: Eerdmans, 2008, especially pages 133–60.

Levison, John R. *Filled with the Spirit*. Grand Rapids: Eerdmans, 2009, especially pages 366–421.

Lieu, Judith M. *I, II, & III John: A Commentary*. NTL. Louisville: Westminster John Knox, 2008.

Lincoln, Andrew T. *Truth on Trial: The Lawsuit Motif in the Fourth Gospel*. Peabody, MA: Hendrickson, 2000.

Thomas, John Christopher. "The Johannine Epistles." Pages 250–56 in *A Biblical Theology of the Holy Spirit*. Edited by Trevor J. Burke and Keith Warrington. Eugene, OR: Cascade, 2014.

Thompson, Marianne Meye. *The God of the Gospel of John*. Grand Rapids: Eerdmans, 2001, especially pages 145–88.

———. *John: A Commentary*. NTL. Louisville: Westminster John Knox, 2015, especially pages 318–22.

Chapter 7

The Holy Spirit in the Letters of Paul

The letters of the apostle Paul, the earliest writings that survive from the period of Christian origins, offer profound theological reflection on the Holy Spirit. These letters represent Paul's attempts to intervene in the specific challenges facing household-based churches for which he was the founding missionary. (Romans is the only letter Paul sent to a church others had started.) The letters are "persuasion events"[1] in which Paul develops sometimes sophisticated rhetorical arguments to deliver theological and ethical teaching. He seeks to guide the churches he has left behind as he extends his mission to other cities in the eastern Mediterranean region of the Roman Empire.

Letters from Paul?

The seven letters generally acknowledged as coming from Paul are 1 Thessalonians, 1 and 2 Corinthians, Galatians, Philippians, Philemon, and Romans. The authorship of six letters within the Pauline tradition is debated: 2 Thessalonians, Colossians, Ephesians, and the trio often labeled Pastoral Letters—1 and 2 Timothy and Titus.

In the course of Paul's response to whatever presenting issues confront him, he describes the work of the Spirit in a variety of ways, each

99

modulated to speak a relevant message to the particular circumstance. Five of the seven letters generally agreed to be written by Paul include significant treatments of the Holy Spirit: 1 Thessalonians, 1 and 2 Corinthians, Galatians, and Romans.[2] I will organize the discussion by letter, drawing attention to the distinctive themes as Paul develops them in each letter. While Paul often uses the word *pneuma* (*spirit*) to refer to a quality of the human being (e.g., a "gentle spirit" in 1 Cor 4:21 or the holiness in spirit of marriage partners in 1 Cor 7:34), our concern in this chapter is the Holy Spirit, the Spirit of God.

First Thessalonians

Probably the earliest of the letters of Paul, 1 Thessalonians is addressed to a small group of recent converts from polytheistic religious practice—worship of idols, as Paul puts it in 1:9, reflecting his Jewish perspective—living in the city of Thessalonica in Macedonia. It is a letter of encouragement for Christ believers who are experiencing hostility from their neighbors because of their new religious commitment (1 Thess 2:1-2, 14; 3:1-10), and who are also distressed because of the deaths of some among them (4:13-18).

In a thanksgiving section beginning at 1:2 (a prayer of thanksgiving ordinarily follows the opening greetings in a Pauline letter), Paul links the activity of the Holy Spirit to the initial preaching of the gospel (lit., *good news*) message to the Thessalonians and to their reception of that message with faith and joy (1:5-6). Paul preached convincingly, and with power, because of the Spirit, and the same Spirit inspired joy in the Thessalonians despite the hostility they immediately encountered.

Paul associates the Holy Spirit not only with believing, joyful reception of the good-news message but also with faithful living that accords with their initial response of faith. In a section of the letter that seeks to nurture mutual fidelity between sexual partners and a commitment of community members to act lovingly and responsibly toward others (4:1-12)—in a word, holiness (or sanctification)—Paul associates this ethic of integrity and care with the divine gift of the Holy Spirit. To reject that divine equipping for holy and honorable living is to spurn this gift from

God (4:8). What Paul only hints at here he will more fully affirm elsewhere (e.g., Rom 8:1-17): the Holy Spirit as God's gift is a divine presence that empowers the moral life. God is able to effect a holy life for the whole person—human spirit (and soul and body) attuned to the divine Spirit (5:23).

Finally, as in the prophetic tradition in Jewish scriptures (see ch. 2 above) and as in the book of Acts (ch. 5 above), 1 Thessalonians 5:19 connects the Spirit and prophetic activity (also in 1 Cor 12:10). Paul urges that the Spirit not be "suppressed," and that means, among other things, not scorning the message of the community's prophets (understood to be speaking at the Spirit's prompting), though discernment in evaluating what prophets declare is still necessary (1 Thess 5:20-21).

First Corinthians

Spirit (*pneuma*) is a prominent term in Paul's first letter to the Corinthians: of the forty occurrences of the word, more than half appear in just two passages, nine in 2:1-16 and twelve in 12:1-13 (then another seven in ch. 14). This is a Spirit-gifted audience, and the accent on the Spirit reflects both that giftedness and the problems that it has generated, centering on conflict within the community of Christ followers in the important, bustling Greek-and-Roman city of Corinth in the province of Achaia.

Do Paul's Letters Address Individuals or Communities?

Many twenty-first-century readers are shaped by their culture to assume that the Bible directs its message to individuals.

It is helpful, though, to realize that Paul's letters were originally written to and for communities of Christ followers.

The letters often use the second person plural *you* [*all*].

The letters would first have been heard by the gathered members of the household-based groups.

As in 1 Thessalonians 1:5-6, Paul links his initial proclamation of the gospel with the activity of the Spirit (1 Cor 2:4). However, Paul places the accent differently; here he emphasizes that the message is not a matter of human wisdom but, instead, Spirit-power. Human faith, and the good-news message that evokes it, spring from and rest in divine power, not an orator's eloquent brilliance (2:1-5). So Paul concludes a passage in which he has argued that the power of the cross defies human wisdom and calculations of strength, but it is God's saving power nonetheless (1:18–2:5). As the argument proceeds in 2:6-16, however, Paul makes clear that the Spirit *does* teach a kind of wisdom; indeed the Spirit discloses the deep mysteries of God. The Spirit mediates divine revelation (also in 2 Cor 3:1-18). Just as one can know what is authentically human only by the human spirit, so only the divine Spirit can teach the things of God. The Spirit reveals this wisdom, yet only those who are tutored by the Spirit can understand the spiritual gifts with which they are endowed (1 Cor 2:12-14). So a community that is marked by the Spirit of God has "the mind of Christ" (v. 16). It may be the deep mysteries of God, but the mind of God—the wisdom of God revealed by the Spirit—is seen in the cruciform pattern of Jesus's life. Spirit as power does not nullify or diminish the strange, paradoxical saving wisdom of the cross. The cross of Jesus means a fundamental shift in perceiving and knowing for people of faith, and the Spirit plays a key role in effecting that shift.[3]

Paul presents the Spirit as a community-shaping force in 1 Corinthians, a letter that forges a strong bond between theology and ethics. The Corinthian body is the holy dwelling place of the holy God (3:16), and much of the letter appeals to the audience to live like it! The Spirit is God-present, residing within the body (both individual and corporate); united to the Lord, one becomes "one spirit with him," and the human body (individual and corporate) is a temple of the Holy Spirit, so that one belongs to another: the Lord (6:17, 19). Formerly, life was plagued by corruption, but now the Corinthians have been washed, sanctified, and justified in the name of the Lord Jesus and in the Spirit of God (6:11). The Spirit is the effective agent of transformation in the Corinthian community. Conduct in the community matters; this is a group called to a holy life that reflects the character of God. The Holy Spirit, God's dynamic presence, is the engine (and, as we will discover, the navigator) for ethics.

Chapters 11–14 address an array of concerns relating to the worship practices of the Corinthian house churches, with particular attention in 1 Corinthians 12–14 to the exercise of spiritual gifts. Not all actions credited to Spirit-inspiration are beneficial. Indeed, Paul begins by imagining an extreme case, probing the limits of claims to be speaking/acting under the impulse of the Holy Spirit (12:1-3): to claim Spirit inspiration for speech that curses Jesus is obviously absurd. By contrast, speech (and therefore faith) that honors Jesus as Lord is the work of the Spirit. As in Galatians 5 (see below), the Spirit plays a decisive role as prompter for faith. The ensuing discussion of the gifts entrusted by the Spirit to the community numbers discernment of spirits among these endowments. Not every claim to the Spirit is in fact holy. For Paul, discernment of the spirits, including prophetic assertions, means that "spirituality can and must be measured by the effects in the ethical realm"—by "the concrete effect upon church life."[4]

E Pluribus Unum and a Capable Community: Diverse Gifts from the One Spirit

Reinforcing unity that values diverse expressions of Spirit-giftedness, Paul gives a selective list of what Spirit-people can do in 1 Corinthians 12:4-11:

communicate wisdom

communicate knowledge

express faith (or faithfulness: *pistis*)

heal

work miracles

speak prophetically

discern spirits

speak in various kinds of tongues (probably regarded as the language of angels; 13:1)

interpret (making meaningful the unintelligible speech in tongues)

All these gifts of the Spirit are to promote "the common good" (v. 7), and all come from one-and-the-same Spirit (vv. 4, 11). And all are to be enacted in love (12:31b–14:1).

In 12:7-13, Paul enumerates nine gifts that the Spirit animates: wisdom, knowledge, faith, ability to heal, (other) miracles, prophetic speech, discernment (assessment) of spirits, speech in tongues, and the interpretation of speech in tongues. In addition, in 7:34 Paul dares to propose that his own apostolic teaching displays that he has the Spirit of God, and in 14:32 he refers to the "spirits of the prophets." This selective listing suggests the diversity of the gifts, which must all be honored. Notice that the tongues-speech so prized by some Corinthians comes last, the reverse of their valuing of it. But Paul also emphasizes that the "one Spirit" of God is the source of each and every gift that builds up the community and its faith/faithfulness. The unity of the community, in all its rich diversity of work and gift, has its source in the Holy Spirit, in the holy, powerful presence of God. The Spirit animates the gifts of individuals but it is also—and especially—God's presence guiding and empowering the whole community of believers for their life together and in the world. This one Spirit initiates (via baptism) a unified community that embraces not only diverse gifts but also cultural difference: "We were all baptized by one Spirit into one body, whether Jew or Greek, or slave or free, and we all were given one Spirit to drink" (12:13; cf. Gal 3:28). Here Paul employs water as a metaphor in two senses: washing (baptism) and drink. Hence, the activity of the Spirit brings both external cleansing and interior transformation. Paul images the church as Christ's body (1 Cor 12:12-31), a culturally diverse group in which the Spirit of God has taken up residence.

In chapter 14, Paul offers specific, practical directions for the worship gatherings of the Corinthian Christ believers. Picking up a thread from 2:6-16, Paul maintains that speech in tongues signals mysteries that are disclosed though the Spirit (14:2). But while this kind of ecstatic speech can benefit the individual, what matters most to Paul is speech and other acts that benefit the group. Gifts from the Spirit serve above all to build up the community (14:12).

Finally, in an expansive discussion in 1 Corinthians 15, Paul proposes to Corinthians who are disposed to view resurrection in purely spiritual terms, disconnected from the body, the image of a "spiritual body." The image does not denote a non-material body but a continuing existence under the control of the divine Spirit. Paul imagines embodied selves transformed by God's life-bestowing Spirit for a permanent sharing in God's life. In this transformation for eternity, Paul offers Christ as a "second Adam" who "became a spirit that gives life" (15:45; cf. the Lord as Spirit in 2 Cor 3:17-18). The first Adam received divine breath and sprung to life; the second Adam—the Christ raised from the dead by God—becomes the agent of the divine spirit-gift of life.

Second Corinthians

After Paul sent 1 Corinthians, conflict within and among the house churches in Corinth morphed into intense conflict between the Corinthians and Paul. Second Corinthians responds to a complex circumstance of estrangement, distrust (fomented by interloping teachers, whom Paul sarcastically labels "super-apostles" in 11:5), and vigorous efforts at reconciliation. An embattled Paul seeks to win back the confidence and loyalty of churches he had organized. In such a turbulent correspondence, Paul returns again and again to the image of the Spirit. As Moyer Hubbard puts it, in 2 Corinthians we see Paul's view of the Holy Spirit "being hammered out on the anvil of conflict."[5]

Second Corinthians: One Letter or Many?

The canonical 2 Corinthians is complex! Because of the twists and turns and dramatic shifts in mood, many scholars think that parts of two or more letters have been incorporated into this edited correspondence.

Two proposals:

Furnish (2005, 35–48) divides into two letters, chs. 1–9 and chs. 10–13

Boring (2012, 254–65) sketches a composite of five letters:

2 Corinthians 8: the collection

2 Corinthians 2:14–7:4: first defense

2 Corinthians 10:1–13:12: severe letter

2 Corinthians 1:3–2:13 + 7:5-16 + 13:11-13: reconciliation

2 Corinthians 9: resuming the collection

An early mention of the Spirit in 2 Corinthians 1:22 pictures it as the sign and seal of God's unqualified yes to us in Jesus Christ, a pledge or first installment (*arrabōn*) of the future full realization of God's promise (1:19-22). Paul picks up this thread in 5:1-5, where he expresses robust confidence in God's commitment to "clothe" with enduring life persons presently subject to physical deterioration and death. The Spirit is again the "down payment" (2 Cor 5:5; cf. Rom 8:23). In a fashion typical of 2 Corinthians, Paul is on the defensive; his profound theological affirmation in 1:22 is framed by a vigorous defense against criticism prompted by a change in his travel plans (vv. 15-18, 23-24). Likewise, a cluster of references to the Spirit in chapter 3 merges theological claim and Paul's need to explain and defend himself. In this instance the issue concerns the value of self-commendation and letters of endorsement (3:1-3; cf. the image of self-commendation in 5:12).

Echoing prophetic texts in Jeremiah and Ezekiel that locate God's activity in relation to the human heart, Paul proposes that the Corinthians are themselves Paul's letters of recommendation, written not on tablets of stone (echoing the commandments given to Moses; see Exod 34:28-35) but on the heart, and not with ink but with the Holy Spirit (2 Cor 3:2-3; cf. Jer 31:33; Ezek 11:19; 36:26). The contrasts Paul draws between stone tablets and the human heart, and between ink and Spirit, initiate an extended rhetorical argument in which the apostle reflects on the life-giving potency of the new covenant in Christ (2 Cor 3:4-18). Paul associates the old covenant and its letter, sponsored by Moses, with elusive and temporary glory, veiled revelation, condemnation, and death. The Spirit-animated ministry of a new covenant, by contrast, delivers permanent, direct, and life-granting experience of the transcendent glory of God. The human creature, though bearing the divine image, does so with a faded glory due to the realities of sin, corruption, and mortality. The Spirit plays a key role here as life-bearer and agent of transformation "from one degree of glory to the next degree of glory," so restoring the *imago Dei* (image of God) in and for which humans were created (v. 18).

This is in some respects an obscure argument, and it has the potential of fostering supersessionist readings in which the "Christian" new-covenant revelation replaces the Mosaic covenant with Israel. Within the context of Paul's rhetorical moves to effect reconciliation with Corinthian Gentile converts, however, 3:12-18 offers a picture of the Spirit as a master interpreter who guides the community toward a perceptive reading of scripture—of Moses and of the divine glory seen now in Christ, who is the Lord-Spirit. Authentic freedom comes with clear thinking and a full apprehension of the divine presence ("glory") now available in Christ: "The

Lord is the Spirit, and where the Lord's Spirit is, there is freedom" (2 Cor 3:17).

Jesus, Lord and Spirit

In 2 Corinthians 3:17-18, readers encounter an unusual coalescing of the names Lord (= Christ) and Spirit:

Paul identifies the Lord as the Spirit

Similar language appears elsewhere in Paul's letters:

Philippians 1:19 – the Spirit of Jesus Christ

Galatians 4:6 – the Spirit of the Son (though here the cry "Abba" indicates that the relation to God as parent is shared with believers)

It is the Spirit that effects this clear vision of the glory of God-in-Christ, a point emphatically expressed with the merging of the identities of the terms *Lord* and *Christ*. Elsewhere, Paul typically describes the activity of the Spirit (of God) as distinct from the identity and role of Christ, the Son of God. Yet the fluidity and flexibility in Paul's use of the language is intriguing; the raw materials for later trinitarian doctrinal thinking are present in the Pauline letters, but not yet a systematic theology of the Spirit.

Fittingly, Paul concludes the letter on this triadic, proto-trinitarian note: "The grace of the Lord Jesus Christ, the love of God, and the fellowship of the Holy Spirit be with all of you" (13:13). This sign-off is no empty rhetoric. The identity and status of the Corinthian Christ followers are now defined by the gracious favor and love of God known in Christ and by their communal participation (*koinōnia*: sharing or fellowship) in the Holy Spirit. The ambiguity of the final image of *koinōnia*—a fellowship with the Spirit or effected by the Spirit?—invites reflection on the way in which theology and ethics cohere in Paul's letters. The life together of the Corinthian house churches can and should enact the love and grace and sharing with which God has gifted them. The Holy

Spirit is the dynamic presence that constructs the bridge from theology to ethics.

Galatians

In Galatians, an angry apostle addresses recent converts from polytheistic religious practice and culture who are being urged by other teachers, in his absence, to submit to the rite of circumcision (if male) and to observe some other laws of Moses (likely food restrictions, feast days, and Sabbath observance). Paul views this as a repudiation of his authority, his mission, and his gospel, so he vigorously defends both his leadership and his gospel, which has emphasized faith, not law-keeping by Gentile converts. In the course of Paul's argument for faith, not works of law, chapter 3 invokes the image of the Spirit. Paul appeals to the Galatians' experience of the Spirit in connection with their conversion (3:2-5). The Spirit was instrumental in their initial reception of Paul's message (faith) and was also operative in experiences of power (*dynameis*, miracles, such as acts of healing). His point is that trust (faith), not law-keeping, opens up access to God's power (Spirit). In a list of the "fruit" produced by God's Spirit, chapter 5 reinforces the link Paul has forged between faith and Spirit: *pistis* (faith or faithfulness) is among the fruits the Spirit produces (5:22). And 5:5, too, ties faith to Spirit, but now pointing faith (rather than law-keeping) toward the future attainment of right standing with God ("righteousness"); the Spirit sustains the hope needed in the meantime. Romans will amplify this hope-nurturing activity of the Spirit (chs. 5 and 8).

Fruitful Spirit in Galatians 5

What does Spirit-life look like? Paul gives a vivid picture in Galatians 5:22-23 of the sort of fruit the Spirit produces:

love

joy

peace

patience

kindness

goodness

faithfulness (or faith: *pistis*)

gentleness

self-control

These qualities are the very opposite of the picture of a life that is destructive of both self and social well-being in 5:20-21.

Galatians draws a sharp either-or opposition between faith and law-keeping, and between Spirit and flesh. Paul links reliance upon law-keeping to slavery and to participation in "flesh"—circumcision thus serves as a metonym for a larger ethical domain, one characterized by a way of life that does not square with the purposes of God. Opposed to the operation of "flesh" is the Spirit (Gal 5:16-17; 6:8; cf. 4:29; Rom 8:2-14; Phil 3:3).

Metonym: What Does That Stand For?

Writers sometimes use a word or image that points to a larger field of ideas, so that this larger network of meanings is evoked by the single word. This is called a metonym. Here is a contemporary example: If someone says, "Give me a hand," they are not asking me to cut off my hand. They want all of me to help them.

In Galatians, Paul can use the specific image of circumcision to conjure the wider notion of "flesh," which figures in the argument of the letter as a descriptor for life dominated by patterns that run counter to the divine purposes for human flourishing.

In Galatians 5, as he will again in Romans 8:1-17, Paul employs the metaphor of life as a journey (walking) to depict the Spirit as a force that directs the moral conduct of believers (5:16; the verb *peripateō*, "walk," is translated "live" in the NRSV, obscuring the metaphor; cf. the CEB translation "be guided"; 5:25 does speak of living by the Spirit). On this life's "walk," the Spirit leads and guides (5:18, 25). No law is necessary to rein in the qualities the Spirit generates: "love, joy, peace, patience, kindness, goodness, faithfulness [or faith], gentleness, and self-control" (5:22-23). For Paul, it is God, present as the Holy Spirit, who animates faithful living; theology fuels ethics. The outcome, for those who walk or live by the Spirit (or, shifting the metaphor, who sow a crop to the Spirit), is eternal life (6:8).

Romans

Romans, addressed to Christ believers in a half-dozen or more household-based churches in the empire's most important city, is a magisterial expression of Paul's theological vision. It is crafted, in part, to garner the endorsement and support of an increasingly important Christian group, as Paul draws up plans for a future mission to the Iberian peninsula (15:22-33). Also, he seeks to strengthen a community in which the gospel takes concrete shape in a people that is diverse yet unified—bridging cultural distance and especially overcoming the division between Jewish and Gentile Christ believers (14:1–15:13).

Of the thirty-four mentions of *pneuma* (s/Spirit) in Romans, nearly two-thirds occur in chapter 8 (twenty-one times). Here, amplifying points scored more briefly in Galatians, Paul highlights the role of the divine Spirit as (1) the source and empowerment for the moral life and (2) the sustaining presence of God that fosters persevering hope despite deep suffering.

The Holy Spirit in Romans

Spirit as source and power for the moral life

Spirit as the hope-engendering presence of God, even in the reality of suffering

After an extended discussion in Romans 6–7 of the incapacity of God's good gift of the law (Torah) to deliver human beings from the dominating power of sin, and thus from condemnation and death, 8:1 pivots decisively to affirm that there "isn't any condemnation for those who are in Christ Jesus." Why this dramatic turn? Because "the law of the Spirit of life in Christ Jesus" has liberated from "the law of sin and of death." But this is not and cannot be simply a liberation *from*. The divine Spirit experienced in connection with Jesus Christ can generate righteousness and thereby give the life toward which the Torah, though ineffectually, pointed (8:3-4). In 8:2-14 (as in Galatians 5), Paul contrasts two modes of life. One is dominated by the flesh—here depicted as creaturely rebellion against the divine purpose (Rom 8:7), not simply as finitude and contingency—and thus by sin and death. The other is ruled by the Spirit. Those who "walk" (v. 4 NRSV), are (v. 5), and set their mind (v. 6) in sync with ("according to," *kata*) the Spirit will know life and peace (v. 6). They will live in a manner that fulfills the law's just demand (v. 4), that is marked by the "rightness" that issues in life (v. 10). Paul is confident that his Roman audience is "in the Spirit," that "God's Spirit lives" in them (v. 9). In the same verse he identifies this divine Spirit as also the Spirit of Christ, and asserts that participation in ("having") the Spirit of Christ indicates that one belongs to him.

Verse 11 returns to Paul's more customary way of referring to the Spirit: it is the Spirit of the one (= God) who raised Jesus from the dead and who also resides in believers and thus gives life even to their mortal bodies. As in 1:4, Romans 8:11 associates the Holy Spirit (or, in phrasing that appears only in 1:4 in Paul's letters, the "Spirit of holiness") with the resurrection of Jesus. First for Jesus (as first fruits), then for believers, it is through the agency of the Spirit that God beckons the life of the future into the present. Romans 8:13 then frames the point of verses 4 and 10 (those who live by the Spirit do what is right and just) in terms of cosmic warfare: one must put to death the body's acts in order to live.

But how, if the cosmic powers of sin and death are so potent? Tweaking the metaphor of walking in or by the Spirit, 8:14-17 pictures believers being led by the Spirit of God. The Spirit, however, is not experienced simply as an external force acting on believers, for it—that is, God's empowering presence—now resides within them. And under the Spirit's guidance, their status has been fundamentally changed, from a spirit of slavery to that of adopted children who share the inheritance with Christ. Those who are led by the Spirit of God are God's own sons (and daughters) and so coheirs with Christ. The promise is sure: the Spirit seals recognition of the believer's status as God's adopted child. Nevertheless, experience of the Spirit is (shifting metaphorical fields) a matter of first fruits, not the final harvest; the redemption of (mortal) bodies that are now embedded in a yearning, suffering cosmos is still future. Full adoption as God's children, in this ultimate sense, is still awaited (8:23). In the meantime, the Spirit, mediating God's holy and life-sustaining presence, stands with believers, prays with and for them, and makes known to them God's benevolence (8:26-27)—God's unqualified yes to the human creature, as 2 Corinthians 1:19-20 puts it, no matter what happens (Rom 8:28-39). God's bountiful love is known at the deep core of one's being ("poured out in our hearts") through the gift of the Holy Spirit (5:5).

Paul's Eschatological Vision

Eschatology, from the Greek word *eschaton* (end or last), has to do with ideas and expectations about the end time. Paul adopts and adapts an apocalyptic eschatological view from his Jewish heritage: the present is an age of rebellion and evil that will give way (soon!) to a future age that God will bring. However, for Paul the future has already broken into, or invaded, the present, reclaiming it for God's life-giving purposes. The resurrection of Jesus and the activity of the Holy Spirit are two decisive markers of this fundamental "turn of the ages" that has already occurred, though its completion still awaits.

As in 2 Corinthians (1:21-22; 5:5), Romans 8:23 pictures experience of the Spirit as an advance sharing in the future life of God—anticipatory, yet a matter of experience and thus a basis for confidence about participation in the glorious future God will bring.[6] For Paul, as for other New Testament writers, the Holy Spirit is an eschatological (end-time) gift—an encounter with God's saving, powerful presence now, even on this side of the final completion of God's purposes. Like the resurrection of Jesus (1 Cor 15:20, 23), experience of the Spirit is the first installment that ensures an eventual full share—whether as *arrabōn*, "down payment," with the rest sure to follow (2 Cor 1:22; 5:5), or as *aparchē*, "first crop" of the full harvest, which will come soon (Rom 8:23). In Paul's panoramic, cosmic vision in Romans 8, not the individual alone, and not the believing community alone, but the whole creation—the whole universe—by hope moves toward a future glory that will far surpass even the most intense suffering of the present age. In Romans 5 and 8, the Spirit undergirds hope through the experience of loss and suffering; it mediates God's presence in sustaining strength and nurturing love (5:5; 8:23, 26-27; also 15:13). The Spirit prays with and for the believer when words fail (8:26-27; cf. v. 15: the Spirit's prompting prayer "Abba, Father"; also in Gal 4:6).

Spirit as Pledge and First Fruits: Living into the Future Now

Paul uses two metaphors that bring the future into the present, as anticipation of the future reality:

arrabōn—down payment, first installment, or earnest money (2 Cor 1:22; 5:5)

aparchē—first fruits of the harvest, with the rest expected soon (e.g., Rom 8:23)

A number of other passages in Romans mention the Holy Spirit. In 9:1 Paul invokes the Holy Spirit as witness that he is speaking truth when he expresses his anguish at the situation of his fellow Jews in their resistance to the gospel message. Romans 11:8 then appeals to scriptural memory that God gave a rebellious people a spirit that prevents the sight and hearing that would save them (drawing from Isa 29:10 and 6:9-10)—the very opposite of the Holy Spirit as prompter of faith (as, e.g., in Gal 5:22). Later, Paul claims that the power of signs and wonders—the power of God's Spirit—confirms Paul's bold proclamation of the gospel of Christ (15:19). In a section of the letter (14:1–15:13) that responds to what Paul regards as unnecessary tensions between Jewish and Gentile believers sparked by cultural differences, 14:17 offers the triad of "righteousness, peace, and joy in the Holy Spirit," not differing practices relating to food and drink, as the key markers of God's reign. And Paul pictures the Holy Spirit as the instrument whereby God receives as holy (sanctified) the offering of the Gentiles that is a primary aim of Paul's mission (15:16). Finally, through the Lord Jesus Christ and the love that comes from the Spirit, Paul requests prayer on his behalf as he prepares to take the collection to Jerusalem (15:30-31).

Paul's Collection for Jerusalem

Often in Paul's letters, the apostle mentions a collection of funds from his Gentile churches in Galatia, Achaia, and Macedonia to aid the (Jewish) Christ believers based in Jerusalem:

1 Corinthians 16:1-4

2 Corinthians 8–9

Romans 15:25-28

The implication of Romans 15:30-31 appears to be that Paul is apprehensive that this offering from his churches will be rejected at Jerusalem.

In two places, Paul aligns the human spirit with the divine Spirit, portraying a quality of human life that contrasts with a way of living that has been left behind. He commends circumcision of the heart, *en pneumati* (in s/Spirit; NRSV: spiritual), not letter (2:29), a figurative circumcision that does not exclude Gentiles. And 7:6 speaks of service in the newness of the s/Spirit, not in the oldness of the legal code, in its captivity to the flesh and sin (cf. Phil 3:3; 2 Cor 3:1-18). It is the Spirit of God that liberates the human person for a life-nourishing, hope-sustaining existence.

Paul and Beyond: Ephesians

Before drawing together significant discoveries in this chapter's exploration of the Holy Spirit in the letters and theological vision of the apostle Paul, it is fitting to pause to consider the development of Spirit imagery in Ephesians. This letter, though attributed to Paul, is likely from another author who a generation or so after Paul adds his own voice to the canonical collection of Pauline letters. Ephesians offers a robust theological exposition (chs. 1–3), followed by elaboration of its practical, ethical implications (chs. 4–6). Linking the two large sections of the letter is a vigorous affirmation of God's gracious and effective initiative in Jesus Christ to overcome division in the human family, particularly between Jews and Gentiles (2:1-22). This affirmation provides the theological basis for the author's appeal to the Christ-believing audience—the body of Christ—to live in unity, by love for one another (4:1-16).

Tasting the Future Now

The image of a pledge or down payment (*arrabōn*) appears also in the undisputed Pauline letters in 2 Corinthians 1:22; 5:5 (see the discussion of 2 Corinthians above). Experience of the Spirit draws the future into the present, fostering confident trust that a full, enduring participation in the life and glory of God will surely come.

The Holy Spirit is a significant presence spanning both the theological claims in chapters 1–3 and the ethical-parenetic moves in chapters 4–6. The Spirit has an instructional role as an agent of divine revelation: the Spirit gives wisdom (1:17) and reveals to apostles and prophets alike the previously hidden mystery of God's saving work in Christ (3:5). The disclosure of this deep mystery conveys a message of assurance, for the Spirit "seals" the promise of an enduring inheritance. This "seal," the Spirit, is a pledge or first installment, received even now, of the full inheritance sure to be enjoyed (1:13-14). Already in the present, the Spirit mediates access to God as "Father," access available to both Jews and Gentiles (2:18). Ephesians associates the Spirit with imagery of power, the riches of (divine) glory, and the very fullness (*plērōma*) of God (3:16, 19). Despite the provisional, partial character of the *arrabōn* image, therefore, the Spirit does not convey divine presence and power in an incomplete way but points instead to the full majesty, power, and splendor of God.

Parenesis: Moral Instruction in Paul's Letters

The letters of Paul contain extensive moral teaching, often called parenetic instruction, from the Greek word *parenesis*. Letters like 1 Thessalonians, 1 Corinthians, and Philippians are permeated by parenetic teaching, interwoven with theological argument. Often, though, Paul structures letters so that specific directions for the practical life of the audience come in the last major part of the letter. Examples include Galatians 5–6, Romans 12:1–15:13, and Ephesians 4–6.

The heady theological affirmation of Ephesians 2 culminates in the picture of the believing community as a holy house of God, constructed *en pneumati*: "in" or "by" the Spirit (v. 22). This imagery prepares for the parenetic appeals, or instructions for faithful living, that follow in chapter 4. Verses 2-3 of this chapter open an extended summons to readers to embody concretely the unity that God has effected through the death of Christ. The verses offer the image of one body that encompasses all God's redeemed people across religious, ethnic, and cultural barriers (the claim of ch. 2). This one body is animated by one Spirit. As in 1 Corinthians 12 and Romans 12 (see the discussion of these letters above), Ephesians employs the body metaphor to call the church to unity, though in a more generic fashion. The one Spirit signifies God's unifying presence in and among God's diverse-but-one people. The image blends unity and diversity as well as divine activity and human response.

These positive appeals to unity in Ephesians 4:1-16 yield to negatively framed admonitions in 4:17-32. This passage seeks to distance the audience from the corrupt and corrupting practices stereotypically ascribed to Gentiles. In this connection, the author charges readers not to "grieve the Holy Spirit of God" (v. 30 NRSV), echoing the language of Isaiah 63:10. This admonition is tied to the image of divine Spirit as "seal," picking up the reassuring motif from Ephesians 1:13 but now scoring the point that faith's assurance does not mean a guarantee without regard to faithful performance. The Spirit signals divine sealing for a *future* day of redemption—of freedom restored.

In a lengthy series of exhortations to wise and faithful conduct, the author urges readers to be filled not with intoxicating wine but in (or with or by; Greek: *en*) the Spirit (5:18; cf. the Pentecost Spirit outpouring and the assumption of intoxication in Acts 2:13, rebutted by Peter in 2:15-21, 33). What does one under the influence of the divine Spirit say and do? The effects of Spirit-filling are seen and heard in spiritual songs that praise and give thanks. The Spirit composes the tunes and lyrics of doxology (Eph 5:18-20).

Ephesians pictures the present age as an arena of fierce struggle with potent, menacing forces of evil still abroad in the world. The defensive armor by which believers are equipped for combat in this arena includes the piercing sword of the Spirit, which is none other than the very word of God (cf. Heb 4:12; Rev 1:16; 19:13, 15). The Spirit arms the believing community not with an implement of violent destruction but with the penetrating wisdom from God that exposes evil for what it is. In the difficult circumstances in which people of faith find themselves in the present, with all its lures toward unfaithful performance, they will be steeled by prayer "in the Spirit" in every season and circumstance (Eph 6:18).

Summary

The texts surveyed in this chapter indicate the importance of the Holy Spirit in Paul's experience, in his rhetorically crafted letters to his churches, and in his theology. In ways that respond to the particular circumstances of a letter's audience, Paul's language of the Spirit highlights several themes. Spirit does many things for Paul.

In tandem with the resurrection of Jesus, the Spirit signals that the present, though an era in which adversity and suffering persist, is nevertheless a time in which the power of the future—the re-creative, restorative power of God—is already at work. The Spirit is pledge and promise of the future available to experience even now, and therefore a basis for confident hope, even in the midst of suffering. This assurance is grounded in the love and grace of God, whose powerful presence in the Spirit energizes, informs, and sustains prayer.

Moreover, the Holy Spirit is also both guide and source of power for the moral life. As such, it is the antithesis to the self- and other-destructive life dominated by the flesh (or by sin). It is also contrary to the attempt to fund ethics from law-keeping. The Spirit equips and empowers the believer to enact love and fulfill the justice (righteousness) toward which the law points—a capacity to live faithfully etched by the Spirit on the human heart, as prophetic oracles from Jeremiah and Ezekiel pictured. So God gives faith and faithfulness, and thereby facilitates right-relation of humans to the divine. The Spirit mediates these gifts.

This equipping for a life well lived is both personal and corporate. Attention to the ways in which the Spirit funds a diverse array of spiritual gifts within the community of believers well displays this connection between personal and communal. Paul insists that diverse gifts of the Spirit contribute to the health and effective functioning of the community and are therefore to be welcomed and embraced. These include flashier gifts of ecstatic and prophetic speech and miracles of healing, even if Paul must temper the over-enthusiasm of some Corinthians for tongues and prophecy. But Spirit-giftedness is also evident in less dramatic abilities and tasks, crucial to the church's life and mission: teaching, preaching, and organizational leadership. Knowledge and wisdom, cultivated through study and much effort, are also crucial Spirit-gifts, yet here too claims to superior wisdom that set some above others in the group contradict the character of the gospel. Whatever the gift, legitimate expression of it strengthens the whole group through loving care for the other. This is what the Spirit looks like in action.

For Further Reading

Atkinson, William P. "1 Corinthians." Pages 146–59 in *A Biblical Theology of the Holy Spirit*. Edited by Trevor J. Burke and Keith Warrington. Eugene, OR: Cascade, 2014.

Boring, M. Eugene. *An Introduction to the New Testament: History, Literature, Theology*. Louisville: Westminster John Knox, 2012.

Brown, Alexandra R. *The Cross and Human Transformation: Paul's Apocalyptic Word in 1 Corinthians*. Minneapolis: Fortress, 1995.

Burke, Trevor J. "Romans." Pages 129–45 in *A Biblical Theology of the Holy Spirit*. Edited by Trevor J. Burke and Keith Warrington. Eugene, OR: Cascade, 2014.

Clark, Matthew. "Pastoral Epistles." Pages 213–25 in *A Biblical Theology of the Holy Spirit*. Edited by Trevor J. Burke and Keith Warrington. Eugene, OR: Cascade, 2014.

Cousar, Charles B. *The Letters of Paul*. IBT. Nashville: Abingdon, 1996.

Dunn, James D. G. "Galatians." Pages 175–86 in *A Biblical Theology of the Holy Spirit*. Edited by Trevor J. Burke and Keith Warrington. Eugene, OR: Cascade, 2014.

Fee, Gordon D. *God's Empowering Presence: The Holy Spirit in the Letters of Paul*. Peabody, MA: Hendrickson, 1994. Repr., Grand Rapids: Baker, 2011.

———. *Paul, the Spirit, and the People of God*. Peabody, MA: Hendrickson, 1996.

Furnish, Victor Paul. *II Corinthians*. AB 32A. New York: Doubleday, 1984. Repr., New Haven: Yale University Press, 2005.

———. *The Theology of the First Letter to the Corinthians*. NTT. Cambridge: Cambridge University Press, 1999.

Hubbard, Moyer, "2 Corinthians." Pages 160–74 in *A Biblical Theology of the Holy Spirit*. Edited by Trevor J. Burke and Keith Warrington. Eugene, OR: Cascade, 2014.

Levison, John R. *Filled with the Spirit*. Grand Rapids: Eerdmans, 2009, especially pages 253–316.

Meyer, Paul W. *The Word in This World: Essays in New Testament Exege-*

sis and Theology. Edited by John T. Carroll. Louisville: Westminster John Knox, 2004, especially pages 117–32.

Munzinger, André. *Discerning the Spirits: Theological and Ethical Hermeneutics in Paul*. SNTSMS 140. Cambridge: Cambridge University Press, 2007.

Rabens, Volker M. "1 Thessalonians." Pages 198–212 in *A Biblical Theology of the Holy Spirit*. Edited by Trevor J. Burke and Keith Warrington. Eugene, OR: Cascade, 2014.

———. *The Holy Spirit and Ethics in Paul: Transformation and Empowering for Religious-Ethical Life*. 2nd ed. Minneapolis: Fortress, 2014. Orig. monograph WUNT 2/283. Tübingen: Mohr Siebeck, 2010.

———. "Power from In Between: The Relational Experience of the Holy Spirit and Spiritual Gifts in Paul's Churches." Pages 138–55 in *The Spirit and Christ in the New Testament and Christian Theology: Essays in Honor of Max Turner*. Edited by I. Howard Marshall, Volker Rabens, and Cornelis Bennema. Grand Rapids: Eerdmans, 2012.

Turner, Max. "Ephesians." Pages 187–97 in *A Biblical Theology of the Holy Spirit*. Edited by Trevor J. Burke and Keith Warrington. Eugene, OR: Cascade, 2014.

Yates, John W. *The Spirit and Creation in Paul*. WUNT 2/251. Tübingen: Mohr Siebeck, 2008.

Chapter 8

The Holy Spirit in First Peter, Hebrews, and Revelation

Beyond the Gospels, Acts, and the letters of Paul, the Holy Spirit (or Spirit of God) figures in important ways in the other letters and in the Apocalypse of John (book of Revelation). Space does not permit a comprehensive treatment, but this chapter will sketch the presentation of the Spirit in the books of 1 Peter, Hebrews, and Revelation. Each of these writings addresses a setting that is defined in large measure by cultural conflict, whether with the Jewish tradition (esp. Hebrews) or with Greco-Roman culture and the reality of Rome's imperial rule (esp. 1 Peter and Revelation).

- In 1 Peter, the Spirit radically reframes the values of identity and honor, and of the meaning of life amidst suffering and death. This presentation of the Spirit speaks to an audience that has experienced disruption and cultural dislocation as a consequence of Christian commitment.

- Hebrews presents the Holy Spirit as an authoritative, divine voice heard in scripture, bearing witness to the establishing of a new and effectual covenant through Christ. The Spirit is also that scriptural voice's interpreter. Moreover, the Spirit is an eternal and gracious reality in which believers share but dare not presume belongs to them without consideration for their manner of living.

- Revelation addresses a situation in which Christ believers disagree about how to conduct themselves as people faithful to God-in-Christ within the Roman Empire: should they engage or retreat from the structures and practices of the empire? In this setting, the Spirit inspires the prophetic witness of John and underscores its divine origin and authority. Although other spirits are prompting counterfeit claims to power and sovereignty (Rev 13:15; 16:13-14; 18:2), John's all-seeing, sevenfold Spirit of God informs an alternative vision of authentic rule. The Spirit fosters hope among readers whom the book summons to persevering, courageous witness to the sovereignty of God, as well as disengagement from the empire.[1]

First Peter

First Peter, addressed to "God's chosen strangers in the world of the diaspora, who live in Pontus, Galatia, Cappadocia, Asia, and Bithynia" (all of these regions located in Asia Minor, within present-day Turkey), carries the authorial identifier "Peter, an apostle of Jesus Christ" (1 Pet 1:1). The authorship of the letter is uncertain, although it certainly invokes the authority and tradition associated with the eminent apostle Peter.[2] The audience tag "strangers in the world of the diaspora" is instructive, as this letter speaks to the reality of cultural dislocation in Roman imperial space.[3] Communities addressed by the letter are experiencing hostility and adversity because of their new religious commitment as "Christians." The author encourages persevering loyalty to Jesus Christ and a response to hardship that is shaped by his model of non-retaliatory trust in the God from whom authentic honor comes (e.g., 2:7, 21-25; 4:13-19). Under intense pressure in the world, a people gifted and empowered by the Spirit become an alternative temple, a sacred space and people: "spiritual temple...a holy priesthood" who "offer up spiritual sacrifices that are acceptable to God through Jesus Christ" (2:5).

The connection between suffering and honor ("glory," *doxa*: 1:11) in God's provision of salvation is already part of the ancient testimony given to God's people. The biblical prophets conveyed this message, speaking in concert with the divine Spirit, whether described as the "Spirit of Christ" (v. 11) or "the Holy Spirit, who was sent from heaven" (v. 12). The Holy Spirit not only guides the message and the interpretation of scripture but also empowers the people of God to be holy themselves—set apart in a distinct, alternative pattern of living within the largely polytheistic Greco-Roman culture—and thus to reflect the character of the holy God. Just as God "who called you is holy," the author admonishes readers to "be holy in every aspect of your lives... [as it] is written, You will be holy, because I am holy" (1:15-16; the phrasing quotes from Lev 11:44-45; 19:2). So the quality of life evident within the believing community shows the human spirit aligned with the divine Spirit:

- gentleness of spirit ("the enduring quality of a gentle, peaceful spirit [which] is very precious in God's eyes," addressed to women believers in 1 Pet 3:4)

- unity, compassion, and humility ("be of one mind, sympathetic, lovers of your fellow believers, compassionate, and modest in your opinion of yourselves," in 1 Pet 3:8)

The last three Spirit references in 1 Peter reframe the painful present experience of suffering in terms of the assurance of future honor and life with God. A poetic fragment that the author borrows from early Christian tradition affirms that Christ, though he suffered and was "put to death," was "made alive by the Spirit [or, in the spirit]" (3:18). And this was not just about his own life; precisely "in the s/Spirit" he visited "the spirits in prison" (v. 19), bringing a message of good news and hope to persons (or spirit-beings assumed to inhabit the space between earth and heaven) who once lived but were not obedient to God (v. 20).[4] The Spirit has a part here in the resurrection of Christ and his installation in a position of heavenly glory and power (vv. 21-22), and also in extending the benefits of righteousness and life to others, even those who were unrighteous.

Who Are the "Spirits in Prison"?

Who are the imprisoned spirits whom Jesus Christ visits after being raised to life in/by the Spirit (1 Pet 3:18)?

Possibilities include these:

all the dead (cf. 4:6)

the wicked contemporaries of Noah who perished in the flood (Genesis 6–8)

the rebellious angels of Genesis 6:1-6, as developed in Jewish apocalyptic writings such as 1 Enoch (chs. 6–16) and Jubilees (5.6; 7.21; 10.1-9)—spiritual beings (= angels, as in Heb 1:14) possibly confined in the zone between earth and heaven.

First Peter 4:6 picks up this thread, affirming that even dead persons who have been judged (by God) have a share in Spirit-life after the pattern of God's own life: "Indeed, this is the reason the good news was also preached to the dead. This happened so that, although they were judged as humans according to human standards, they could live by the Spirit [or, in the spirit] according to divine standards." As in 3:18, the Greek phrasing is ambiguous; it is difficult to distinguish between life in the Spirit (life enabled by God's Spirit) and a quality of human life (alive in spirit). Since spirit-life has its source in divine empowerment, which also shapes personal and communal living, perhaps it would be a mistake to force a choice between *spirit* and *Spirit* in such cases.

Finally, 4:14 transposes the "Spirit of God" image into the honor/glory key. Followers of Jesus who are maligned precisely because they carry "Christ's name" will enjoy divine blessing: "the Spirit [or, spirit] of glory —indeed, the Spirit of God—rests on" them. The present reality entails suffering as a result of Christian commitment, yet the author urges his audience toward persevering loyalty and fidelity, confident that they will follow Jesus's own path from suffering to honor. The glory that the Spirit of God resting on believers will convey does not mean that their suffering will simply vanish. But it is not the last word; it is not ultimate. God's gift of life and honor, through the Holy Spirit, will both nurture faithful, holy living and nourish persevering hope.

Hebrews

The anonymous "letter" to the Hebrews—by its own self-presentation a "message of encouragement" (13:22), an example of early Christian preaching—includes several intriguing references to the Holy Spirit. In this late-first-century CE writing that weaves together robust christological reflection on the significance and work of Jesus, bold readings of Jewish scripture, and stern moral appeals for fidelity to Christian commitment, the Spirit and its activity have an important part. The appeals are vigorous, evidently because the first reading communities have not sustained the seriousness and enthusiasm of their initial commitment.[5]

Agency of the Holy Spirit as Authorial Voice and Interpreter of Scripture

As we have discovered, New Testament writings often credit the Holy Spirit with an instrumental role in the crafting of authoritative messages in scripture (e.g., Matt 22:43; Mark 12:36; Acts 4:25; 1 Pet 1:10-12). Hebrews goes even further. It assigns the voice heard in scripture directly to the Holy Spirit, without mention of a human mediator. And it casts that voice in the present tense ("says," "testifies"; 3:7; 10:15 NRSV)—thus speaking to the author's own time and to that of every audience subsequently.[6] The Spirit is both the author of the inspired message within scripture (3:7-11; 10:15-17) and its interpreter (9:8).[7] Moreover, the interpretive view attributed to the Spirit elides with that of the author of Hebrews (e.g., in 9:9). Hebrews weaves into an almost seamless robe scriptural quotations or echoes and interpretive commentary that draws the christological and moral-parenetic implications. So readers are hard pressed to disentangle the authoritative voice of the Spirit and the creative, reflective activity of the author. This is a rhetorical strategy designed to enhance the authority of this message of encouragement.

Hebrews 3:5-12 invokes Psalm 95:7-11 to undergird an appeal for persevering, unswerving fidelity to the living God on the part of believers who are members of God's own household, over which Christ is positioned as a faithful son (v. 6). The Holy Spirit redirects the "today" of Psalm 95:7 to the situation of the audience of Hebrews, and the message and its stakes are clear. The promise of entry into the divine "rest" (Heb 3:11)—of a share in the eternal salvation to which God has opened access in Christ—is still held before the believing community, but only if they persist in faith and hope. To turn away from the living God, as the wilderness generation did, is to invite disaster.

Hebrews 9:1-28 takes us from the wilderness tent/tabernacle to the heavenly sanctuary, from the establishing of a (first) covenant that was not effective in producing an obedient people to the institution of a new covenant that rests on a permanently effective sacrifice. This sacrifice, that of Jesus, decisively deals with human sin and restores the human heart and human action. In constructing this argument, the author draws extensively from the narrative about the wilderness tent/tabernacle (Exod 25:1–31:11; 36:1–40:38) and especially from the depiction of the high priest's role in the ritual of the Day of Atonement (Lev 16:1-34). Into this narrative web is inserted a claim that the Spirit teaches about the limited efficacy of the atonement ritual undertaken by Israel's high priest. The fact that it deals only with the priest's own sin and with sins "the people committed in ignorance" (Heb 9:7) means that it cannot be a comprehensive or enduring answer to human sin: "With this, the Holy Spirit is showing that the way into the holy place hadn't been revealed yet while the first tent was standing" (9:8). Christ, however, *has* appeared as a high priest (v. 11) who has "entered the [true, heavenly] holy of holies once for all" (v. 12). There, "he offered himself to God through the eternal Spirit as a sacrifice without any flaw" (v. 14). So a new covenant has been established (cf. 8:7-13), one that provides access to an eternal inheritance (9:15). The one who shares in the very being of God (1:3) also shares in the eternal, divine Spirit and can convey a share in an eternal, heavenly inheritance.

Chapter 10 amplifies this christological portrait, and does so by again invoking the Holy Spirit's witness in scripture. After completing his once-for-all-time, atoning sacrifice in the true (heavenly) sanctuary, Christ "sat down at the right side of God," and "since then he's waiting 'until his enemies are made into a footstool for his feet'" (Heb 10:12-13, quoting Ps 110:1). The sacrifice is effective once for all because its outcome is a people made holy (Heb 10:14), a people fit for the heavenly Jerusalem as "spirits of the righteous who have been made perfect," as 12:22-23 puts it.

The author then turns to the covenant-restoration promise of Jeremiah 31 to frame Christ's achievement in establishing this new covenant. The prophet's message to this effect is the direct witness of the divine Spirit: "The Holy Spirit affirms this when saying, 'This is the covenant that I will make with them. After these days, says the Lord, I will place my laws in their hearts and write them on their minds. And I won't remember their sins and their lawless behavior anymore'" (Heb 10:15-17; emphasis removed). Here the author quotes from Jeremiah 31:33-34 and Ezekiel 36:26-29; 37:14. These passages picture the divine Spirit, rather than the law and capacity to keep it, being placed within Israel. The author spells out the implication of the divine resolve to forget the people's sins: "When there is forgiveness for these things, there is no longer an offering for sin" (v. 18). Exactly this state of affairs, the author of Hebrews is convinced, pertains in the enduring covenant God has brought into being through Christ: forgiveness of sins is granted and no additional sacrifices are necessary. The Holy Spirit is an ancient witness, but a timeless one, as this voice continues to speak through scripture to the present of the book's audience. And what the Spirit places in first-person speech is actually the speech and action of God. Yet the magnitude of the divine mercy is no reason for false assurance and complacency, as the rest of chapter 10 makes clear.

Eternal Spirit, Spirit of Grace

What Hebrews 9:14 calls the "eternal Spirit," 10:29 brands the "Spirit of grace." And by this point the author has repeatedly emphasized the merciful grace of God, who in Christ's sacrifice once-for-all provides forgiveness. The Spirit of grace, God of grace, indeed. The other side of the coin, however, is the prospect of severe judgment for any who after receiving the gift of forgiveness persist in sin and rebellion, living in a way that shows contempt for the gift of divine mercy: "How much worse punishment do you think is deserved by the person who walks all over God's Son, who acts as if the blood of the covenant that made us holy is just ordinary blood, and who insults the Spirit of grace?" (10:29). Vengeance and judgment are the divine prerogative (v. 30), so "it's scary to fall into the hands of the living God!" (v. 31). Again here, we find in tandem interpretation of scripture and theological claim as the basis for vigorous moral-parenetic appeal. Hebrews urges its audience not toward presumption of grace but, instead, toward perseverance in faithful living in response to grace.

Sharing in the Spirit and the Character of the Life of Faith

The eternal, divine Spirit is not simply an external force operating outside humankind but an experienced reality in which believers participate. Beyond the work of remembering and interpreting scripture, already discussed, there is also special activity such as "signs, amazing things, various miracles [or powerful deeds]," as well as gifts or "gifts from the Holy Spirit," through which God attests the salvation provided through Christ (2:1-4). Again, in the activity of the Spirit, God's hand is seen, though the specifics of the gifts it activates remain unmentioned (in contrast to 1 Cor 12:4-11).

Again here, the author accents the importance of continuing to live as people who participate in the divine Spirit: "Because it's impossible to restore people to changed hearts and lives who turn away once they have seen the light, tasted the heavenly gift, become partners with the Holy Spirit, and tasted God's good word and the powers of the coming age. They are crucifying God's Son all over again and exposing him to public shame" (6:4-6). Theological claim and moral-parenetic appeal are wedded once more. The "Father of spirits" (12:9)—of believers as God's own children—disciplines them "for a little while," so that they "can share [God's] holiness" (12:10). God's Holy Spirit is fashioning a people who share in the divine holiness. Suffering and adversity, therefore, do not signal shame but, on the contrary, the divine commitment to the covenant people's life. Through the challenges they face today, God's people have a share in the divine Spirit, the power of the future breaking into the present and sustaining trust in God's promise even against the evidence of sight and experience (ch. 11). So the Spirit contributes meaningfully to this book's "message of encouragement [and admonition]" (13:22).

Book of Revelation

"I was in a Spirit-inspired trance [lit., in the spirit, or in the Spirit]" on the small island of Patmos, the visionary John tells us (Rev 1:10), and this writing presents his provocative prophetic witness to the sovereignty of God and his co-regent Jesus Christ in a world that Rome thinks it rules. The phrase *en pneumati* ("in the Spirit") colors the whole book and its many visions as a Spirit-inspired prophetic message (1:10; 4:2; 17:3; 21:10). This last New Testament writing, the final one to be discussed in this book, comes from a time of crisis late in the first century CE, likely toward the end of the reign of Domitian (emperor 81–96 CE). What is the situation on the ground? Active imperial persecution of Christians is probably not a current reality in John's time, though it is a not-so-distant memory (Nero's persecution of Christians at Rome was in 64 CE). Persecution will become a threat just a couple of decades later in nearby regions in Asia Minor, as evident in the exchange of letters between Pliny the Younger (the governor of Pontus and Bithynia) and the emperor Trajan in 112–113 CE.[8]

Yet the visionary prophet John can see the writing on the wall; indeed, in this social setting, his sharp witness to a *kyrios* (Lord) other than the emperor is politically provocative. He sends this genre-blend of prophecy, apocalypse, and letter to the Christian groups in the Roman province of Asia (western Asia Minor, or twenty-first-century Turkey). John perceives an inevitable collision between two world systems and two contradictory loyalties: imperial Rome and the one true God. God exercises dominion in the most improbable, counter-imperial of ways, through the Lamb slaughtered—Jesus, the faithful witness, crucified (1:5; 5:1-14). John seeks to recruit other faithful witnesses who will tell that truth, disengage from Rome's corrupt and corrupting political-economic-religious system, and face the consequences. The courageous martyr-witness of Antipas in Pergamum (2:13) may be the harbinger of things to come. This is the sharp prophetic testimony John brings to bear on a contested question within the churches known to him: how should they engage—or *not* engage—the imperial world?

Prophetic Testimony in the Spirit

John delivers a spirited message, one that in various formulations he credits to the Spirit of God. John's first-person narration reports the experience of visions (including both sight and sound) in a trance-like ecstasy *en pneumati* (in the Spirit) that transports him (in imaginative perception) so that he can see (and hear) reality from a heavenly perspective (1:10; 4:2; 17:3; 21:10). As a visionary, his experience of the Spirit therefore involves a "suspension of normal consciousness," but not at the expense of John's agency or of his intellectual acuity and deep knowledge of the Jewish scriptures.[9]

John frames chapters 2–3 as letters dispatched to the *angeloi* (the angels or messengers) of seven churches in cities in the Asian province, hence to the whole church of that part of the empire (the number seven symbolizes completeness, here and elsewhere in Revelation, drawing upon a rich scriptural heritage).[10] Each of these letters is cast as the risen Jesus's word of commendation, encouragement, and warning—the tone of the message adjusted to fit the situation of the church, as John assesses it. At the close of the letters, Jesus urges the recipients to listen well: "If you can hear, listen to what the Spirit is saying to the churches" (2:7, 11, 17, 29; 3:6, 13, 22). So the voice of the risen Jesus is delivering the message of the Spirit to the church. But since the voice of Jesus-and-Spirit is conveyed by the (Spirit-inspired) prophet, John is laying claim to a divine source for his prophetic teaching.

John's claim to prophetic inspiration by the Spirit in such a striking, ecstatic manner is more a theological claim than a psychological one; the concern is less "to describe *how* he received the revelation [than] to *communicate* it to his readers."[11] John appeals to visionary experience *en pneumati* (in the Spirit) to point to God as the source of the witness he is providing.

The Spirit also sees to it that John goes where he needs to go to receive the revelation in sight and sound that he is to convey: heaven to see the real throne room (4:2); a desert to spy a woman and beast symbolizing Babylon, soon to fall (17:3); and a high mountain to glimpse the descent of heavenly Jerusalem (21:10). Extraordinary transportation aided by the Spirit is a motif Revelation shares with many other writings (e.g., Acts 8:39-40; 1 Kgs 18:12; 2 Kgs 2:16; Ezek 3:12, 14; 8:3; 11:1, 24; 37:1; 43:5).[12]

The intimate relation between Jesus and the Spirit is reinforced in the letter to Sardis (3:1-6): "These are the words of the one who holds God's seven spirits and the seven stars" (v. 1). Jesus is speaking here, and John pictures him as one who has (hence directs or controls) the seven spirits of God, symbolic representation of the fullness of the divine Spirit. The sevenfold Spirit appears four times: 1:4, where they appear before the throne of God; 3:1, paired with seven stars; 4:5, again in front of the throne of God, and identified also as "seven flaming torches"; 5:6, once more in front of the throne, this time identified also as the slaughtered Lamb's "seven eyes, which are God's seven spirits, sent out into the whole earth" (echoing Zech 4:10). The imagery is evocative and fluid, a kaleidoscope-like presentation of images—seven spirits = eyes = torches (lamps)—all associated both with the heavenly throne, hence with authentic power, and with Jesus Christ or the Lamb, hence with power as faithful witness-unto-death. The Spirit sees, knows, and reveals all.

Picking up the image of "seven flaming torches" or lamps and drawing from the depiction of seven lampstands and two olive trees in Zechariah 4:1-6, Revelation 11:3-13 presents the forceful public testimony of two witnesses. They have extraordinary power reminiscent of Moses and Elijah (vv. 5-6) but eventually succumb to the beast-driven powers of rebellion against God (vv. 7-10). The breath (or spirit: *pneuma*) of life from God, however, revives them and they ascend to heaven (v. 12). In a fashion typical of Revelation, the symbol-rich imagery is fluid and kaleidoscopic. These two witnesses are pictured as two olive trees and also as two lampstands, among the seven lampstands already associated in Revelation 1:20 with the seven churches of Asia that John is addressing. So the two witnesses stand for the public testimony to which the whole church is called.

The intertextual play with Zechariah 4, along with the image of life-restoring breath/spirit from God, points through the bold testimony of the prophetic church to the divine Spirit. For, in the words of Zechariah's revealing-interpreting angel, explaining the two olive stands the prophet sees, "This is the LORD's word to Zerubbabel: Neither by power, nor by strength, *but by my spirit*, says the LORD of heavenly forces" (Zech 4:6, emphasis added). It turns out that the Spirit of God is also powerful—resurrection-life potent. Here is reason for the church to which John speaks to sustain its prophetic witness, even when the cost is great.

View of the Future—for the Present Moment

The activity of the Spirit giving divine authentication to the prophetic witness of John, and of the prophetic church as a whole, also has much to do with a future not yet experienced, though John can "see" it coming. As in other New Testament writings, with prompts from texts like Joel 2:28-32; Jeremiah 31:31-34; and Ezekiel 37:1-14, the Spirit is an eschatological force, an image of God's future, impinging on and reshaping present reality (e.g., Acts 2:17-21; Rom 8:23; 2 Cor 1:21-22; 5:5).

Revelation articulates a fervent hope for Christ's return and the completion of God's purposes in the world, with the fall of "Babylon"/Rome (ch. 18), the final defeat of the tenacious forces of evil (chs. 19–20), and the descent of an expansive New Jerusalem from heaven to earth (21:1–22:5) as focusing images. In the last chapter of the book, an angel-revealer, the risen Jesus, and the Spirit-inspired prophet form a chorus offering assurance regarding the imminent realization of this hope.

> Then he [the angel] said to me, "These words are trustworthy and true. The Lord, the God of the spirits of the prophets, sent his angel to show his servants what must soon take place." (22:6)

> [Then Jesus adds:] "Look! I'm coming soon. Favored is the one who keeps the words of the prophecy contained in this scroll." (22:7)

[And finally:] "I, John, am the one who heard and saw these things."... The one who bears witness to these things says, "Yes, I'm coming soon." (22:8, 20)

For hard-pressed believers, or those whom John expects soon to face peril because of their witness to God-and-Christ as Lord, the Spirit offers a reassuring message. Once again John gives voice to the divine Spirit: "The Spirit and the bride [the holy city, New Jerusalem] say, 'Come'" (22:17a). This divine message will call for response: "Let the one who hears say, 'Come!' And let the one who is thirsty come! Let the one who wishes receive life-giving water as a gift" (22:17b). John taps the promise of Isaiah 55:1: the gift of life-sustaining water for all who will come to drink. Earlier, the Spirit in tandem with another voice from heaven has promised blessing to all who persevere in fidelity to God:

> This calls for the endurance of the saints, who keep God's commandments and keep faith with Jesus. And I heard a voice from heaven say, "Write this: Favored are the dead who die in the Lord from now on." "Yes," says the Spirit, "so they can rest from their labors, because their deeds follow them." (Rev 14:12-13)

Despite the reality or prospect of present adversity—even death—because of faithful witness to God's sovereignty, readers are assured of ultimate blessing. That is, if they persevere in their courageous witness, their actions will be remembered.

As a prophet, John claims to speak a Spirit-prompted message. Against all the evidence of ordinary sight in the Roman world, he unveils the future that God will surely bring. But the future unveiled is primarily about the present, in the first instance about the situation confronting John's audience in the late first-century CE empire. As Bauckham has so well put it, the Spirit is "constituting the Christian churches [as] the community of the age to come."[13] The point of John's prophetic witness is not to predict the future but "to enable [readers] to see their present from the perspective of the future."[14] The Spirit is a major factor in John's *seeing and hearing* from that divine perspective, in his boldly communicating it to his contemporaries—and in its rediscovery by later generations of readers. In the spirit of John's book, its audience both ancient and present will courageously live by that strange, counterintuitive, and counter-imperial truth. The prophetic message John delivers to the *church* now becomes its prophetic message to the *world*.[15] As with the Spirit-animated dual witnesses of 11:3-13—emblematic of the witness entrusted to the whole people of God—it potentially carries grave danger, but also the promise of transformational, resurrection-powered life.

John's Apocalypse removes any confusion about who is worthy of worship. Even heaven-sent angel-revealers redirect reverence to the one to whom it is owed. Authentic witness of/to Jesus in the form of Spirit-animated prophetic teaching is, in the end, about worship: "Then I fell at his [the angel-revealer's] feet to worship him. But he said, 'Don't do that! I'm a servant just like you and your brothers and sisters who hold firmly to the witness of Jesus. Worship God! The witness of Jesus is the spirit of prophecy!'" (19:10). The humorous irony of the scene underscores the point: worship is rightly given to God alone, not to *any* other being or power, not even mighty emperors or exalted angels. Spirit-inspired prophetic teaching summons John's audience to authentic worship, in concert with countless others who gather around the one legitimate throne in praise of God and of the Lamb (chs. 4–5).

As we have discovered, the divine Spirit contributes to the two primary practical and rhetorical aims of Revelation: encouragement (or assurance) and challenge (or warning). The stakes are high, and the Spirit moves prophets like John to summon believers to persevere in their courageous witness to the rule of God-in-Christ, confident that the future belongs not to Rome and its emperor (or their successors in later eras) but to the God who is sovereign over all the universe and all eternity. In the words of the "letter" opening:

> John, to the seven churches that are in Asia: Grace and peace to you from the one who is and was and is coming, and from the seven spirits that are before God's throne, and from Jesus Christ—the faithful witness, the firstborn from among the dead, and the ruler of the kings of the earth.... "I am the Alpha and the Omega," says the Lord God, "the one who is and was and is coming, the Almighty." (1:4-8)

This is the core message of Revelation. As John might say, "Let anyone who has an ear listen to what the Spirit is saying to the churches." And to Rome (and its successors): note well.

For Further Reading

Attridge, Harold W. *Hebrews: A Commentary on the Epistle to the Hebrews.* Hermeneia. Minneapolis: Fortress, 1989.

Bauckham, Richard. "The Role of the Spirit." Pages 150–73 in *The Climax of Prophecy: Studies on the Book of Revelation.* Edited by Richard Bauckham. London: T and T Clark, 1993.

Blount, Brian K. *Revelation: A Commentary.* NTL. Louisville: Westminster John Knox, 2009.

Boring, M. Eugene. *1 Peter.* ANTC. Nashville: Abingdon, 1999.

————. *Revelation.* IBC. Louisville: Westminster John Knox, 1989.

Carter, Warren. *What Does Revelation Reveal? Unlocking the Mystery.* Nashville: Abingdon, 2011.

Donelson, Lewis R. *I & II Peter and Jude.* NTL. Louisville: Westminster John Knox, 2010.

Elliott, John H. *A Home for the Homeless: A Social-Scientific Criticism of I Peter, Its Situation and Strategy.* Minneapolis: Fortress, 1990. Repr., Eugene, OR: Wipf and Stock, 2005.

Gorman, Michael J. *Reading Revelation Responsibly: Uncivil Worship and Witness; Following the Lamb into the New Creation.* Eugene, OR: Cascade, 2011.

Green, Joel B. "Faithful Witness in the Diaspora: The Holy Spirit and the Exiled People of God according to 1 Peter." Pages 282–95 in *The Holy Spirit and Christian Origins: Essays in Honor of James D. G. Dunn.* Edited by Graham N. Stanton, Bruce W. Longenecker, and Stephen C. Barton. Grand Rapids: Eerdmans, 2004.

Hodson, Alan K. "Hebrews." Pages 226–37 in *A Biblical Theology of the Holy Spirit.* Edited by Trevor J. Burke and Keith Warrington. Eugene, OR: Cascade, 2014.

Johnson, Luke Timothy. *Hebrews: A Commentary*. NTL. Louisville: Westminster John Knox, 2006.

Koester, Craig R. *Hebrews: A New Translation with Introduction and Commentary*. AB 36. New Haven: Yale University Press, 2001.

Levison, Jack. *Inspired: The Holy Spirit and the Mind of Faith*. Grand Rapids: Eerdmans, 2013.

Motyer, Steve. "The Spirit in Hebrews: No Longer Forgotten?" Pages 213–27 in *The Spirit and Christ in the New Testament and Christian Theology: Essays in Honor of Max Turner*. Edited by I. Howard Marshall, Volker Rabens, and Cornelis Bennema. Grand Rapids: Eerdmans, 2012.

Reddish, Mitchell G. *Revelation*. SHBC. Macon, GA: Smyth and Helwys, 2001.

Schafroth, Verena. "1 and 2 Peter." Pages 238–49 in *A Biblical Theology of the Holy Spirit*. Edited by Trevor J. Burke and Keith Warrington. Eugene, OR: Cascade, 2014.

Thomas, John Christopher. "Revelation." Pages 257–66 in *A Biblical Theology of the Holy Spirit*. Edited by Trevor J. Burke and Keith Warrington. Eugene, OR: Cascade, 2014.

Yarbro Collins, Adela. *Crisis and Catharsis: The Power of the Apocalypse*. Philadelphia: Westminster, 1984.

Chapter 9

Trajectories and Themes: Theological Dimensions of the Spirit in the New Testament

The discussion of the Holy Spirit in the New Testament in chapters 4–8 has been thorough, but by no means comprehensive. Even though I have not attempted to touch every base (even more true of the survey in chs. 2 and 3 of important texts and approaches in the Tanak as well as the wider Greco-Roman world), the importance of the subject for readers of the New Testament should be clear. As I bring this book to a close, it may be helpful to draw together significant threads in these chapters, to tease out some theological and ethical implications of the analysis, and to trace just a few of the many paths interpretation of the Holy Spirit has taken over the centuries.

Trajectories

The metaphor of "closing the book" does not suit very well. Within the Bible, and across cultures and eras, talk about and experience of the Spirit suggest instead an openness that resists closure, a creative impulse as people of faith have brought to language the ways in which the sacred— the holy, the divine—interacts with the world, including human society and culture. Within emerging Christian communities, language of the

Spirit was prompted by the ongoing experience of God's presence and activity in life, and this language was encountered over and over again in worship. Contemporary Spirit-prompted "praise worship" of the twenty-first century has antecedents in the earlier history of the churches! Already the Tanak (Old Testament) invited attention to the life-creating, sustaining, and restoring presence of God as Spirit. New Testament authors pick up this thread, tying it closely to the person of Jesus. In him, they were convinced, the divine Spirit was active—a power to proclaim truth, heal the hurting, and call all people to authentic life. Remarkably, they believed they met this Spirit-power in the vulnerability of a man whose life-force was brutally taken from him on a Roman cross.

In ways that pressed insistently toward the paradoxical, early Christ followers attempted to express in language their experience, their conviction that the one God of Israel, creator of all that is, was also encountered in the person of this man from Nazareth—and that beyond his short life he continued to be encountered as a still-living Lord of both church and world. God continued to be encountered, that is, as an enlivening, empowering Spirit-presence. Thus, although the systematic articulation of a trinitarian understanding of God—as one divine being in three distinct "persons"— would arise only in fits and starts in the course of the first three or four centuries of the common era, the raw materials for that development do appear at many places within the New Testament. Here are just four examples:

- Matthew's concluding image of the disciples' charge from Jesus to baptize all nations "in the name of the Father and of the Son and of the Holy Spirit" (Matt 28:19)

- Peter's affirmation in the Pentecost discourse of Acts 2 that Jesus, as exalted Lord, had both received from the Father and poured out on his followers the Holy Spirit (Acts 2:33)

- John's picture of the risen Jesus—the *logos* (Word) who was "with" and also "was" God (John 1:1)—breathing Holy Spirit upon his followers on Easter (20:22)

- Paul's celebration of the diverse spiritual gifts that come from God, Lord, and Spirit (1 Cor 12:4-6)

Voices from the Second and Third Centuries

Reflection on the identity and role of the Holy Spirit, in relation to both God (the Father and creator) and Jesus (the Son), continued in the next two centuries after the documents that would compose the New Testament had been written. Space permits brief mention of just a few of these voices: the *Didache*, Ignatius, Justin Martyr, Irenaeus, and Tertullian.

Didache (*Teaching of the Twelve Apostles*). This early second-century CE manual of instruction guiding the organizing of church life picks up the triadic baptismal formula of Matthew 28:19: baptism "in the name of the Father and of the Son and of the Holy Spirit" (*Didache* 7:1, 3 [AF]). This book also cautions against gullible acceptance of every prophet's claim to be speaking in or by the Spirit (*en pneumati*). The genuine prophet is known by conduct that is consistent with the message spoken: for example, if the "prophet" demands money, he is likely a fraud (ibid., 11:3-12).

Ignatius of Antioch. Among the letters the bishop Ignatius composed and dispatched on his way to martyrdom in Rome (ca. 112 CE), we meet a fascinating blend of metaphors for the interrelationships and functions of Father, Son, and Spirit: the believer is prepared for "the building of God our Father, carried up to the heights by the engine of Jesus Christ, that is the cross, and using as a rope the Holy Spirit" (*To the Ephesians* 9:1 [AF]). Ignatius is also keen to defend the authority of bishops, in service of church unity, and what better appeal can he make than to the Holy Spirit? He credits to the speech of the Spirit the admonition "Do nothing without the bishop...love unity, flee from divisions" (*To the Philadelphians* 7:2 [AF]). Paul's appeal to the Corinthians to let the Spirit fund unity rather than dissension (1 Corinthians 12) lives on in Ignatius's letters, though with the not-so-subtle addition of concern for the bishop's power.

Justin Martyr. Seeking to make an erudite philosophical case in defense of Christian beliefs, the mid-second-century CE apologist Justin Martyr ties the Spirit, God's power, closely to the Word Jesus Christ. In the process, he cites Matthew 1:23 (which is quoting Isa 7:14):

And hear again how Isaiah in express words foretold that He [Christ] should be born of a virgin; for he spoke thus: "Behold, a virgin shall conceive, and bring forth a son, and they shall say for His name, 'God with us.'" For things which were incredible and seemed impossible with men, these God predicted by the Spirit of prophecy as about to come to pass, in order that, when they came to pass, there might be no unbelief, but faith, because of their prediction. (*First Apology* 33:1-2 [ANF])

Justin also emphasizes the activity of the Spirit in informing and animating prophetic teaching (e.g., ibid., 13, 44).

Irenaeus. The writings of Irenaeus, bishop at Lyons (in Gaul, ca. 180 CE), are a rich source of information about the development of Christian theological thought in the last part of the second century, especially in contest with emerging gnostic teachings (featured in Irenaeus's *Against Heresies*). Irenaeus offers a vivid body metaphor to picture the relations among Father, Son, and Spirit: the Son and the Spirit are "God's own hands" (*Against Heresies* 4.20.1). And he associates the Spirit with the figure of Wisdom, present with God prior to creation (ibid., 4.20.3). The Holy Spirit is not a creature but exists before the created world (a dig at the gnostic view of emanations deriving from the divine realm). Moreover, Irenaeus closely associates the Spirit with the church, going so far as to claim that "where the Church is, there is the Spirit of God, and where the Spirit of God is, there is the Church" (ibid., 3.24.1).

Target of Irenaeus's Critique: Gnostic Christianity

Irenaeus levels vigorous, sustained criticism at various expressions of Christian gnostic belief and practice in his five-book treatise *Against Heresies*. Until the mid-twentieth century, the primary source for information about gnostics was to be found in the attacks on it by Irenaeus and other early Christian leaders—scarcely a neutral or sympathetic presentation! With the discovery of a set of manuscripts in the Coptic language from Nag Hammadi in Egypt (1945), scholars can now construct a picture of gnostic ideas apart from the biased accounts by strident critics.

Some of the prominent gnostic ideas:

An emphasis on *gnosis* (knowledge, insight, or intuition) as the key to identity and destiny

A negative view of the world, which is not the creation of the supreme God but the result of error at considerable remove from the divine fullness or *plērōma*

The existence of varying numbers of intermediary entities (*aeons*) between the divine fullness and human life (and also the physical, created world)

A "spark" of divine energy in human beings, who find the path to rescue from this world of imperfection through awareness of their true identity and origin (hence also their destiny)

Ascetic practice (taming or denying the flesh) as the likely enactment of their negative view of the world (though condemned for libertine practices and indulging the flesh)

Tertullian. His career spanning the late second and early third centuries CE, the lawyer-turned-theologian from Carthage (northern Africa) is a particularly fascinating case study with regard to emerging views of the Holy Spirit. His strong inclination toward asceticism was perhaps a factor in his embrace of a Montanist approach in the first decade of the third century. Montanus, active as a teacher in the last third of the second century, emphasized the activity of the prophetic Spirit and distinguished those who were Spirit-filled—including women teachers like Prisca and Maximilla—from the rest of the church. This "new prophecy," as the teaching was called, also had a heightened sense of the imminent approach of the end time; the Paraclete of John's expectation was speaking for the last time in the prophets of this movement. In an essay *Against Praxeas*, Tertullian articulates the relation of the Spirit to God the Father and the Son in a fashion that anticipates important later theological debates: "I believe the Spirit [to proceed] from no other source than from the Father through the Son" (*Against Praxeas* 4 [ANF 3:599]).

Montanus and the New Prophecy

Montanus (active late second century CE) and his followers appealed to the Paraclete as source of their inspired "new prophecy."

Women such as Prisca and Maximilla were among the Paraclete-inspired prophets.

They located the New Jerusalem of Revelation 20–21 in Phrygia (western Asia Minor).

They advocated a rigorous ethic and ascetic lifestyle.

For a time, Tertullian was attracted to the Montanist view, perhaps especially drawn by its moral rigor.

The emerging "great church" rejected the Montanist teaching, but it continued to recruit adherents for several centuries.

Spirit and Trinity: Taming a Mystery?

The conviction that God—the one God of Israel, creator of the universe—was experienced in the dynamic, triadic activity of Father, Son, and Spirit eventually took shape as belief in a triune (one-in-three) God. The classic doctrinal formulation was affirmed at a council in Nicea in 325 CE and then in an expanded Nicene-Constantinopolitan Creed adopted at the ecumenical council at Constantinople in 381 CE, which included the belief that the Holy Spirit is "the Lord and Giver of life, who proceeds from the Father, who with the Father and the Son together is worshiped and glorified, who spoke by the prophets."

Especially in the Latin-language Western circles of what would become the Roman Catholic Church, it was common to bind talk of the Holy Spirit tightly to Christology (reflection on the person and work of Christ). Two centuries after the council at Constantinople, another council convened at Toledo (in Spain) in 589 CE added a word (*filioque*) to the Nicene Creed that would foment bitter conflict between Western and Eastern churches.

In 1014 the liturgy at Rome formally incorporated this wording. A generation later (in 1054), sharp disagreement about this phrase became a major factor in the decisive rupture between Roman Catholic and Eastern Orthodox communions. The offending *filioque* phrase, generally adopted by Western theologians and rejected by Eastern theologians, affirms that the Holy Spirit proceeds not only from the Father but also "from the Son" (*filioque* = Latin for "and [from] the Son"). For theologians of the Eastern churches, the claim that the Spirit proceeds not only from the Father but also from the Son has been regarded as diminishing God the Father and confusing the relations among the three persons of the Trinity. The effect of Western theologians' embrace of *filioque*, by contrast, is a heightened emphasis on the person and significance of Christ. Eastern Orthodox and Roman Catholic churches and theologians continue to disagree about this matter, and differing interpretations of relevant New Testament passages are much in play (e.g., Acts 2:32-33; John 15:26; 20:22).

No Longer a "Third Fiddle": The Flourishing of Diverse Views of the Spirit

The Holy Spirit has never disappeared from the Christian theological landscape. But despite the contentious debates about the *filioque* phrase in the Nicene Creed, it was once common to regard this "third person of the Trinity" as the least-valued member of the triad, less intensively discussed and debated than the Father and the Son. But no longer! Near the end of the twentieth century, Colin Gunton could observe, "Suddenly we are all trinitarians, or so it would seem."[1] In the last half century, countless vigorous, substantive treatments of the Spirit (pneumatology) have appeared, and in every major section of Christianity. Here are only a few of the important contributors to a renewed interest in the Holy Spirit:

- Roman Catholic: Karl Rahner and Yves Congar

- Reformed Protestant: Jürgen Moltmann and Michael Welker

- Lutheran Protestant: Wolfhart Pannenberg and Robert Jenson

- Greek Orthodox: John Zizioulas

- Evangelical Protestant: Donald Bloesch, James D. G. Dunn, and Clark Pinnock

- Pentecostal: Gordon Fee, Frank Macchia, Max Turner, and Amos Yong

- Latin-American liberationist: Leonardo Boff and José Comblin

- Feminist: Elisabeth Johnson and Rebecca Prichard

- African: Allan Anderson

- Asian: Jung Young Lee[2]

Academic theology is one thing. But what about practical Christian living on the street and in the home and in faith communities? The Spirit has been much in evidence there too. Indeed, Pentecostal fervor such as exploded onto the scene with the Azusa Street Revival in Los Angeles, California (1906), is now a global phenomenon, with perhaps half a billion people currently drawn to Spirit-focused expressions of Christianity (whether in Pentecostal groups or in charismatic renewal movements within Protestant or Catholic churches). Especially in Latin America, Africa, and Asia, Pentecostal and charismatic expressions of Christian faith are vibrant and claim large numbers of adherents.[3] In such groups, the accent falls on tangible effects of a "baptism in the Spirit" that accompanies conversion, notably speaking in tongues; on Spirit-power exhibited in acts of extraordinary healing; and on the fervent expectation of Christ's return. Talk and experience of the Spirit among such people is thus no other-worldly affair reinforcing a split between body and spirit but, instead, a matter of lived, embodied spiritual experience that makes a concrete, practical difference in the way life is lived. But does experience of the Spirit necessarily take such dramatic, intense form, whether in tandem with or subsequent to baptism and incorporation into the Christian community? Can others—Catholic, Protestant, and Eastern Orthodox alike—take the Spirit just as seriously, but understand its operation differently?

If the studies of New Testament treatments of the Holy Spirit within these pages are not wide of the mark, there is no single template within the

New Testament, or the Bible as a whole, of the Spirit's presence and work. Rather, a variety of perspectives and portraits appear within the New Testament, and they resist facile co-opting by the preoccupations both doctrinal and practical of later generations of Spirit-interested readers. The very image of Spirit, as Jesus tried to explain to Nicodemus in John 3:8, will ever and again elude the categories and constraints and control of readers, as well as reading communities. To speak of Spirit is, to be sure, to address matters of the heart, soulful human life at its depths. But it is also a corporate, communal concern, not a private, individual one. And as Jack Levison especially has argued persuasively, the gifts and abilities for which the Spirit equips faith communities do not bypass the disciplined intellectual and ethical striving of "people of the Spirit."[4]

A prolific author on matters of the Spirit, Levison speaks with deep concern about a divide he perceives "between Christians who are drawn to ecstatic experiences and those who are rooted in staid and stable experiences."[5] He worries that "Pentecostals, especially those in the Global South, may be drawn to the transport of ecstatic experiences without the counterbalance of virtue and learning" and that "Christians in historic Protestant, Catholic, and Orthodox traditions may lose the penchant for ecstatic experiences as they pursue virtue and learning in a sort of spirit-less void."[6] In a "divide that is developing due to the stagnancy of many mainline denominations and the explosive growth of Pentecostalism," Levison fears the "threat of a global dichotomy in the church"—the division being largely "rooted in whether Christians think the spirit appears in the spectacular or in a steady spirituality."[7] So Levison sees the prospect of two Christianities rather than one.

Can experience of the divine Spirit, and reflection on the meaning of that experience of God's holy presence, inform readers of the New Testament and energize communities of faith, but in a manner that also fosters unity, a unity that embraces difference? Much is at stake in how we read, and how we appropriate, the testimonies to the Spirit within the pages of the Bible. If we read the diverse views of the Spirit in the New Testament, as they pick up and advance perspectives in the Tanak (Old Testament), we may be aided in moving beyond the too-frequent either-or polarities of past tradition:

- Pentecostal tradition's emphasis on postconversion special endowment with spiritual gifts *versus* non-Pentecostal views of the activity of the Spirit defined in more stable terms institutionally, liturgically, and educationally

- Spirit influence framed in terms of ecstatic experience and gifts *versus* Spirit as an accompaniment to intellectual discipline and moral striving

- The Western church's insistence on the *filioque* phrase in the Nicene Creed *versus* the Eastern Orthodox church's vigorous resistance to the inclusion of this phrase

Might the Orthodox view provide a helpful corrective to distorted theological views among many in Western churches that exalt Christology at the expense of pneumatology? The divine presence and activity, that is, are known not only "in the Son" but also in creation, in the story of Israel, and among all peoples—indeed, in the incarnation itself (in narrative form in both Matthew 1 and Luke 1). There is much to learn as well from the Orthodox tradition's emphasis on Spirit-life as participation or incorporation in the very reality and life of God (the ancient notion of *theosis*). And in this regard, the exaggerated emphasis on the distinction between divine and human S/spirits, between creator and creature, among some Protestant theologians (e.g., Karl Barth) might also meet a needed corrective.

Finally, a correlated concern: might a "theology and ethics of the Spirit" benefit from a shift in the balance of concern away from preoccupation with the relation of Spirit to Christ and toward appreciation of the dynamic interaction between divine and human agency and energies? If so, one may keep in creative, tensive play both divine direction and empowerment and human decision and striving—of individual agents and also communities. Attentiveness to the Spirit may thus create the very possibility for constructive change, for moves toward the flourishing of human communities and of the whole earth.

Themes

To take up the language of the Spirit, as it has pulsed through the centuries and across traditions and cultures, is to grapple with important questions of identity, of group definition and belonging, and of practice—including worship, community striving, and ethical commitments. As a serious reader of the New Testament, I propose to conclude this book by illuminating these theological challenges with insights gained from immersion in the Spirit texts of the New Testament. The comments will be brief and only suggestive and I leave their elaboration in the hands of my readers and—may I dare to imagine?—in the creative working of the Holy Spirit.

Holy Spirit: Life Lived in Awareness of the Presence of God

We have discovered that the Spirit is one of the principal ways in which the holy, powerful presence of God in the human story and in human communities comes to expression in the New Testament, with important anticipations already in the Tanak. The psalmist dares to believe that there is no place—not even Sheol, the place of the dead—that God's Spirit-presence cannot reach (Ps 139:7-12). And God's Holy Spirit is the basis for a joyful life lived in tune with the divine purpose (Ps 51:10-12). Paul, too, affirms this confident trust in a gracious God who is a saving presence—even in the midst of adversity and suffering. The Holy Spirit lavishly poured out in the human heart is God's love experienced in the soulful depths of human life (Rom 5:3-5). Even when an anguished sufferer cannot summon words of faith and petition to address to God, the Spirit is as near as breath in wordless groans—God within praying the prayer for the believer (Rom 8:26-27). God searches the human heart, and God knows the "mind of the Spirit," images of divine presence in circumstances that might suggest to an observer untutored by the Spirit the absence of God instead.

149

Holy Spirit: Life Sustained in Hope

Especially in the letters of Paul, the Holy Spirit is an image of disruption, of the future interrupting the course of things in the present, of God's future breaking into the here and now. The Spirit as sign and seal of God's loving presence—of God's yes to humankind—now sustains the people of God in hope of a future participation in the life and glory of God (Rom 5:1-11; 8:18-39; 2 Cor 1:22). So experience of the divine Spirit offers a provisional, though real, sharing in the ultimate reality that is God. It is not the complete story, but it opens up access to a future of promise in a manner that beckons confident trust: it is a pledge or first installment (*arrabōn*) of the future full realization of God's promise (2 Cor 1:19-22; 5:5); it is the first fruits (*aparchē*) of the harvest, a sure sign that the rest of the harvest will follow (Rom 8:23).

Holy Spirit: Life Open to Change and Freed from the Need for Control

With the associated images of breath and wind, both Testaments develop the sovereign freedom of the divine Spirit, beyond domestication or control by humans. As Jesus's night conversation with Nicodemus indicates, this is but an expression of the sovereign freedom of God (John 3:3-8; cf. 4:23-24). When Acts narrates the beginning of a worldwide mission, this sovereign freedom of God—evident in the activity of the Holy Spirit—plays an instrumental role directing the course of the apostolic community's mission. If the followers of Jesus engage in courageous, boundary-transgressing moves to include Samaritans and then Gentiles in the company of God's people, it is not because of human initiative and innovation. Rather, these surprising twists and turns in the plot result from the insistent, persistent prodding of the Holy Spirit (Acts 8:14-17; 10:19-20, 44-48; with reprise in 11:15-18). God's people are challenged to catch up and keep up with what the Spirit—that is, God—is doing in the world. The community-forming Spirit challenges and removes cultural and ethnic barriers to participation in the people of God.

Holy Spirit: Life Empowered for Meaningful Work and Bold Speech

A prominent feature of the Spirit's activity in the New Testament, again picking up important motifs from the Tanak, is the equipping of God's people with an array of gifts and capabilities. In Genesis, the mark of the Spirit in the character of Joseph is heightened wisdom (Gen 41:38-39), a quality that also exhibits Spirit-equipping in the case of the lead character in the book of Daniel (Dan 5:11-12, 14). During the wilderness period following the Moses-led escape from Egyptian enslavement, the Spirit distributes leadership talent among seventy men, each of them bolstered by a share of Moses's special endowment with the Spirit and each (along with two comrades) receiving the gift of prophetic speech (Num 11:16-30). Even the skill of the artisan can be credited to the Spirit's influence (Exod 28:2-3; 31:1-11; 35:30–36:6). Among the gifts activated by the Spirit, in Paul's view, is wise discernment—wisdom and knowledge (1 Cor 12:8), including perceptive appraisal of the value and legitimacy of various gifts claimed to be Spirit-inspired (v. 10). The image of the Spirit as Paraclete in John's Gospel highlights the continuity between the wisdom—the grasp of truth—that Jesus imparts during his ministry and the knowledge his followers carry forward after his death and resurrection (John 14:26; 16:13-15).

In Acts, the accent falls on prophetic witness and on bold speech attesting God's work in the mission of the Messiah Jesus, a mission now extended to all nations in the activity of his followers. This Spirit-prompted speaking furthers Jesus's own prophetic activity, trumpeted in his opening mission statement in the Nazareth synagogue (Luke 4:16-21, with a nod to Isa 61:1-2). And that, too, was but another chapter in a continuing story, as Spirit-prompted speech is prominent in the Gospel's opening chapters (Zechariah in Luke 1:68-79, Simeon in 2:27-35). The motif of Spirit-inspired prophetic speech picks up an important strand from the Tanak's witness to the Spirit (e.g., Joel 2:28-32; Zech 7:12; Neh 9:30; repeatedly in Ezekiel). While some scholars have made exaggerated claims that the Holy Spirit in the Bible *is* the Spirit of prophecy, thus downplaying other important roles played by the Spirit in biblical texts,[8] this is an important theme in both Testaments. Paul certainly includes the capacity for prophetic speech among the gifts for which the Spirit equips the people of God for worship and service (1 Cor 12:10, 28). But Paul argues vigorously in 1 Corinthians 12 that Spirit-animated speech—whether ecstatic tongues-speech or prophetic interpretation—is only one of many marks of the Spirit's presence in the community. Here Paul highlights the diverse spiritual capacities that all derive from the empowerment of the one Spirit—which is to say, from the one God.

Both in 1 Corinthians (chs. 8, 12, 13) and in Galatians (ch. 5), Paul binds the operation of the Spirit in the community of Christ followers to love. Faith, itself the work of the divine Spirit, is enacted in love. This is the concrete expression of the Spirit in human terms. The Spirit, then, ties theology and ethics together: God's presence is evident in the way people treat one another. The Spirit and its gifts are not a private matter for individuals but a communal, relational affair. Also, and more extensively, Romans 8 pictures the Holy Spirit residing within the community and its members as the divine empowerment of ethical living—of faithful response to the gracious initiative of God (Rom 8:1-17). Ezekiel's vision of a faithful people of God empowered by God's Spirit placed within them, and so able truly to *live*, finds new life here (see Ezek 36:22-28; 37:1-14). As in Ezekiel, so too in the letters of Paul this is a vision for communal life, not a private, individualistic one. As Paul puts it in 1 Corinthians 12, the operation of the Spirit is to serve one central purpose: to promote "the common good" (12:7).

Creator Spiritus: Embodied Life Embedded and Renewed on Earth

From Genesis 1 onward, the Bible offers the Spirit—*rûaḥ* or *pneuma*—as a creative force. As Spirit, God calls a world into existence, sustains creaturely life, and in the face of the menacing threat of death and annihilation restores life. Chaos turns to creative order with the active presence of the Spirit-wind of God (Gen 1:2). The human creature receives life-breath or spirit from the creator (Gen 2:7), and when the divine Spirit withdraws, life ceases (Job 27:2-4; 33:4; 34:14-15; Ps 146:3-4). But death, whether of an individual or of a people, does not have the last word.

The Spirit-wind-breath from God returns to restore life, and not just bio-logical or national/corporate existence but also authentic life (Ezek 36:22-28; 37:1-14). This is true of the Messiah, whose life is snatched from him but restored by the divine Spirit in resurrection (Rom 1:4; 8:11). It is true also of God's people, for whom the deterioration and death of physical bodies is not the whole story. A "spirit-body" fitted for eternity by the risen Lord—the "life-giving Spirit" (1 Cor 15:45)—awaits (15:42-57).

To return to the question with which we started in chapter 1: What do we see when we say, "That's the Spirit!"? Among other things, this is what we have discovered in the pages of the New Testament. Life touched by the Holy Spirit

- is lived in awareness of the presence of the holy, the presence of God;

- is sustained in hope even through the experience of adversity and suffering;

- is open to change, new directions, and new possibilities—even challenging conventional and deeply entrenched social, economic, and political arrangements;

- is equipped and empowered for bold action and courageous prophetic speech, informed by wise discernment.

Above all, we see the Spirit in the creating, sustaining, fostering, and restoring of life. Not death, but life is the final word whispered, perhaps sometimes shouted, by the Holy Spirit-breath of the divine into human life and community. That's the Spirit!

For Further Reading

Anderson, Allan H. *Moya: The Holy Spirit from an African Perspective.* Pretoria: University of South Africa Press, 1994.

Barrett, C. K. *The Holy Spirit and the Gospel Tradition.* London: SPCK, 1947.

Bloesch, Donald G. *The Holy Spirit: Works and Gifts.* Downers Grove, IL: InterVarsity, 2000.

Boff, Leonardo. *Holy Trinity: Perfect Community.* Maryknoll, NY: Orbis Books, 2000.

Comblin, José. *The Holy Spirit and Liberation.* Translated by Paul Burns. Maryknoll, NY: Orbis Books, 1989.

Congar, Yves. *I Believe in the Holy Spirit.* Translated by David Smith. 3 vols. New York: Crossroad, 1997.

Dunn, James D. G. *Baptism in the Holy Spirit: A Re-examination of the New Testament Teaching on the Gift of the Spirit in Relation to Pentecostalism Today.* London: SCM, 1970.

————. *Jesus and the Spirit: A Study of the Religious and Charismatic Experience of Jesus and the First Christians as Reflected in the New Testament.* London: SCM, 1975.

Fee, Gordon D. *God's Empowering Presence: The Holy Spirit in the Letters of Paul.* Peabody, MA: Hendrickson, 1994. Repr., Grand Rapids: Baker, 2011.

Gaventa, Beverly R. "Pentecost and Trinity." *Int* 66 (2012): 5–15.

Gunton, Colin. *The Promise of Trinitarian Theology.* 2nd ed. Edinburgh: T and T Clark, 1997.

Jenson, Robert W. *The Triune God.* Vol. 1 of *Systematic Theology.* Oxford: Oxford University Press, 1997.

Johnson, Elisabeth. *Women, Earth, and Creator Spirit.* New York: Paulist, 1993.

Kärkkäinen, Veli-Matti, ed. *Holy Spirit and Salvation: The Sources of Christian Theology.* Louisville: Westminster John Knox, 2010.

Lee, Jung Young. *Trinity in Asian Perspective.* Nashville: Abingdon, 1996.

Levison, John R. *Inspired: The Holy Spirit and the Mind of Faith.* Grand Rapids: Eerdmans, 2013.

Macchia, Frank D. *Baptized in the Spirit: A Global Pentecostal Theology.* Grand Rapids: Zondervan, 2006.

Moltmann, Jürgen. *The Spirit of Life: A Universal Affirmation.* Translated by Margaret Kohl. Minneapolis: Fortress, 1992.

Pannenberg, Wolfhart. *Systematic Theology*. Translated by G. Bromiley. 3 vols. Grand Rapids: Eerdmans, 1991–97.

Pinnock, Clark H. *Flame of Love: A Theology of the Holy Spirit*. Downers Grove, IL: InterVarsity, 1996.

Prichard, Rebecca Button. *Sensing the Spirit: The Holy Spirit in Feminist Perspective*. St. Louis: Chalice, 1999.

Rahner, Karl. *Experience of the Spirit: Source of Theology*. Theological Investigations 16. New York: Crossroad, 1981.

Thiselton, Anthony C. *The Holy Spirit—in Biblical Teaching, through the Centuries, and Today*. Grand Rapids: Eerdmans, 2013.

———. *A Shorter Guide to the Holy Spirit: Bible, Doctrine, Experience*. Grand Rapids: Eerdmans, 2016.

Turner, Max B. *The Holy Spirit and Spiritual Gifts in the New Testament Church and Today*. Grand Rapids: Baker, 1997. Rev. ed. Peabody, MA: Hendrickson, 2005.

Welker, Michael. *God the Spirit*. Translated by John F. Hoffmeyer. Minneapolis: Fortress, 1994. Repr., Eugene, OR: Wipf and Stock, 2013.

Yong, Amos. *The Spirit Poured Out on All Flesh: Pentecostalism and the Possibility of Global Theology*. Grand Rapids: Baker, 2005.

Zizioulas, John. *Being as Communion: Studies in Personhood and Church*. Crestwood, NY: St. Vladimir's Seminary Press, 1985.

Notes

1. "That's the Spirit!"

1. See especially John R. Levison, *Inspired: The Holy Spirit and the Mind of Faith* (Grand Rapids: Eerdmans, 2013).

2. Terence Paige, "Who Believes in 'Spirit'? *Pneuma* in Pagan Usage and Implications for Gentile Christian Mission," *HTR* 95 (2002): 420–34.

3. James D. G. Dunn, *Baptism in the Holy Spirit: A Re-Examination of the New Testament Teaching on the Gift of the Spirit in Relation to Pentecostalism Today* (London: SCM, 1970), 21–22, 54.

4. Ibid.

5. Especially influential has been work by Troels Engberg-Pedersen; see, for example, *Cosmology and Self in the Apostle Paul: The Material Spirit* (Oxford: Oxford University Press, 2010).

6. A helpful, detailed summary of Moltmann's several books addressing the Holy Spirit is available in Anthony C. Thiselton, *The Holy Spirit–in Biblical Teaching, through the Centuries, and Today* (Grand Rapids: Eerdmans, 2013), 400–411.

7. Jürgen Moltmann, *The Spirit of Life: A Universal Affirmation*, trans. Margaret Kohl (Minneapolis: Fortress, 1992), 143.

8. Ibid., 7; emphasis orig.

9. Frank D. Macchia, *Baptized in the Spirit: A Global Pentecostal Theology* (Grand Rapids: Zondervan, 2006), 30, 44; a helpful summary of Macchia's work can be found in Thiselton, *Holy Spirit*, 456–61.

2. The Spirit in Jewish Scripture

1. John R. Levison, *Filled with the Spirit* (Grand Rapids: Eerdmans, 2009), 65.

2. The divine name, in these four letters (transliterated Hebrew letters), often spelled with vowels as "Yahweh." YHWH is commonly translated "Lord" (rendering the Greek equivalent *kyrios* in the LXX) in the CEB and elsewhere.

3. James Edward Robson, *Word and Spirit in Ezekiel*, LHBOTS 447 (London: T and T Clark, 2006), 24.

4. Levison, *Filled with the Spirit*, 87–99.

3. The Spirit in Second Temple Literature and Greco-Roman Culture

1. Levison, *Filled with the Spirit*, 109–17.

2. Arthur Everett Sekki, *The Meaning of Ruaḥ at Qumran*, SBLDS 110 (Atlanta: Scholars Press, 1989), 223.

3. George T. Montague, *The Holy Spirit: Growth of a Biblical Tradition* (New York: Paulist, 1976), 103.

4. Ibid., 109.

5. Levison, *Filled with the Spirit*, 144.

6. Carl R. Holladay, "Spirit in Philo of Alexandria," in *The Holy Spirit and the Church according to the New Testament*, ed. Predrag Dragutinovic, Karl-Wilhelm Niebuhr, and James Buchanan Wallace (Tübingen: Mohr Siebeck, 2016), 342–43.

7. Cited in Levison, *Filled with the Spirit*, 148; see also *Who Is the Heir of Divine Things?* 55–57.

8. Levison, *Filled with the Spirit*, 148.

9. Holladay, "Spirit in Philo," 355. Unless otherwise indicated, translations from Greco-Roman writings in this chapter come from the volumes of the Loeb Classical Library.

10. Ibid., 360; Levison, *Filled with the Spirit*, 158.

11. Levison, *Filled with the Spirit*, 189–96.

12. John R. Levison, *The Spirit in First Century Judaism*, AGJU 29 (Leiden: Brill, 1997), 132–33.

13. Ibid., 32–33.

14. Ibid., 169–70.

15. Paige, "Who Believes in 'Spirit'?," 420–34. The merging of the terms *unclean spirit* and *demon* in Luke 4:33-34 suggests that this author is clarifying that by (unclean) spirit is meant the same thing as demon (*daimonion*) in the customary vocabulary of the Greco-Roman world. See Paige, "Who Believes in 'Spirit'?," 435.

16. Levison, *Filled with the Spirit*, 293.

17. Ibid., 138–39.

18. Ibid., 138.

19. Quoted in Paige, "Who Believes in 'Spirit'?," 426.

20. Levison, *Filled with Spirit*, 139–40.

21. Ibid., 141.

22. Paige, "Who Believes in 'Spirit'?," 427–29.

23. Michael Peppard, *The Son of God in the Roman World: Divine Sonship in Its Social and Political Context* (New York: Oxford University Press, 2011), 113.

24. Ibid., 114–15.

4. The Holy Spirit in Mark and Matthew

1. See John T. Carroll, *Jesus and the Gospels: An Introduction* (Louisville: Westminster John Knox, 2016), 49; M. Eugene Boring, *Mark: A Commentary*, NTL (Louisville: Westminster John Knox, 2006), 14–15.

2. Craig S. Keener, *The Spirit in the Gospels and Acts: Divine Purity and Power* (Peabody, MA: Hendrickson, 1997; repr., Grand Rapids: Baker, 2010), 60.

3. Ibid., 70.

4. On the setting and distinctive literary character of Matthew, see Carroll, *Jesus and the Gospels*, 89–98; Donald Senior, *Matthew*, ANTC (Nashville: Abingdon, 1998), 21–26.

5. Blaine Charette, *Restoring Presence: The Spirit in Matthew's Gospel*, JPTSup 18 (Sheffield: Sheffield Academic, 2000), 78.

6. Ibid., 79.

7. Eduard Schweizer, *The Holy Spirit*, trans. Reginald H. Fuller and Ilse Fuller (Philadelphia: Fortress, 1980), 54.

8. See the analysis in Carroll, *Jesus and the Gospels*, 102–3, 105.

5. The Holy Spirit in Luke-Acts

1. Luke Timothy Johnson, *The Acts of the Apostles*, SP 5 (Collegeville, MN: Liturgical Press, 1992), 14. The fourth-century CE Christian preacher and writer John Chrysostom labeled Acts "The Gospel of the Holy Spirit" (Homilies on Acts 1.5).

2. A listing of the various actions attributed to the Spirit in Luke-Acts appears in William H. Shepherd, *The Narrative Function of the Holy Spirit as a Character in Luke-Acts*, SBLDS 147 (Atlanta: Scholars Press, 1994), 248.

3. See Levison, *Inspired*, 91–123. Craig S. Keener points out that while Acts relates the sign of tongues-speech three times (in chs. 2, 8, and 19), it is not depicted as a necessary accompaniment of Spirit reception. Rather, "Luke reports such phenomena to assure us that these disciples received the Spirit (especially the dimension of cross-cultural empowerment)" (*Acts: An Exegetical Commentary*, 4 vols. [Grand Rapids: Baker, 2012–15], 3:2822).

4. Levison, *Filled with the Spirit*, 365.

5. Emphasized, e.g., in Craig S. Keener, *The Spirit in the Gospels and Acts*, 190; Schweizer, *Holy Spirit*, 57, 76, 78; see also Keener, Acts, 1:523: Luke's focus in Acts is on prophetic-empowerment for mission.

6. On the Holy Spirit as "christological mission director," see Ju Hur, *A Dynamic Reading of the Holy Spirit in Luke-Acts*, JSNTSup 211 (Sheffield: Sheffield Academic Press, 2001), 149.

7. Keener, *The Spirit in the Gospels and Acts*, 194. See also Keener, *Acts*, 1:525: In Acts, "the Spirit guides believers to cross cultural-unity" in a multicultural church (emphasis orig.).

8. Aaron J. Kuecker, *Spirit and the "Other": Social Identity, Ethnicity and Intergroup Reconciliation in Luke-Acts*, LNTS 444 (London: T and T Clark, 2011), 158.

9. Ibid., 167.

10. Ibid., 188; emphasis removed.

11. On this literary technique in Luke-Acts, see Daniel Lynwood Smith, *The Rhetoric of Interruption: Speech-Making, Turn-Taking, and Rule-Breaking in Luke-Acts and Ancient Greek Narrative*, BZNW 193 (Berlin: de Gruyter, 2012).

12. Shepherd, *Narrative Function of the Holy Spirit*, 101.

13. Matthias Wenk, "Acts," in *A Biblical Theology of the Holy Spirit*, ed. Trevor J. Burke and Keith Warrington (Eugene, OR: Cascade, 2014), 122–23, 128; see also Keener, *Acts*, 1:523.

14. Ibid., 122–23; see also Max Turner, *Power from on High: The Spirit in Israel's Restoration and Witness in Luke-Acts*, JPTSup 9 (Sheffield: Sheffield Academic Press, 1996; repr., Eugene, OR: Wipf and Stock, 2015), 391.

6. The Spirit-Paraclete in the Gospel of John and First John

1. The distinctiveness of John's narrative presentation of the public activity of Jesus is captured memorably in the title of a book by Robert Kysar: *John, the Maverick Gospel*, 3rd ed. (Louisville: Westminster John Knox, 2007). Also, see the discussion in Carroll, *Jesus and the Gospels*, 185–86, 192–95.

2. Marianne Meye Thompson, *John: A Commentary*, NTL (Louisville: Westminster John Knox, 2015), 105.

3. Ibid.

4. Adapted from the translation by Gary Burge, "The Gospel of John," in Burke and Warrington, *Holy Spirit*, 107.

5. Levison, *Filled with the Spirit*, 376.

6. Thompson, *John*, 319.

7. Ibid., 320. The text box "Jesus and the Spirit: Parallel Paracletes" borrows with minor adaptation from a table of parallels in Gary M. Burge, *The Anointed Community: The Holy Spirit in the Johannine Tradition* (Grand Rapids: Eerdmans, 1987), 141, with helpful nuance provided in Thompson, *John*, 319–21.

8. Thompson, *John*, 320.

9. Here and below, the references listed to the left of the arrow point to the activity of God, while those to the right of the arrow describe the activity of the Spirit-Paraclete.

10. Ibid.

11. Ibid., 321.

12. See Carroll, *Jesus and the Gospels,* 185–86, 190, 198, 200, 229–30; Andrew T. Lincoln, *Truth on Trial: The Lawsuit Motif in the Fourth Gospel* (Peabody, MA: Hendrickson, 2000).

13. R. Alan Culpepper, *The Gospel and the Letters of John*, IBT (Nashville: Abingdon, 1998), 211–12.

14. Although some scholars propose that one or more of the letters actually preceded the composition of the Gospel (in its present twenty-one-chapter form), I regard it as probable that 1–3 John reflect later developments in the Johannine communities (conceding the possibility that some portions of the Gospel such as ch. 21 represent later additions). On these issues, see M. Eugene Boring, *An Introduction to the New Testament: History, Literature, Theology* (Louisville: Westminster John Knox, 2012), 631–33; Culpepper, *Gospel and Letters*, 48–61. Judith M. Lieu does not find in 1 John clear knowledge of or appeals to the Gospel and maintains that the two independently rework common traditions (*I, II, and III John: A Commentary*, NTL [Louisville: Westminster John Knox, 2008], 8).

15. John Christopher Thomas, "The Johannine Epistles," in Burke and Warrington, *Holy Spirit*, 250.

16. Levison, *Filled with the Spirit*, 407–9.

17. See Lieu, *I, II, and III John,* 174–75.

18. As we will see in ch. 7, Paul also commends testing of the spirits and connects Spirit-prompting to faithful belief and speech about Jesus, specifically as Lord (1 Cor 12:1-3). For Paul, however, the prime evidence of the activity of the divine Spirit is the unity of a diversely gifted

community (1 Cor 12:4-11)—a pragmatic test that the community of 1 John would not pass!

7. The Holy Spirit in the Letters of Paul

1. Paul W. Meyer, *The Word in This World: Essays in New Testament Exegesis and Theology*, ed. John T. Carroll (Louisville: Westminster John Knox, 2004), 114.

2. See the concise discussion of the authorship of these letters in Charles B. Cousar, *The Letters of Paul*, IBT (Nashville: Abingdon, 1996), 165–80, 200–203. The discussion in this chapter is confined to the seven "undisputed-authorship" letters, with particular focus on 1 Thessalonians, 1 and 2 Corinthians, Galatians, and Romans, and also one of the "disputed-authorship letters," Ephesians.

3. See Alexandra R. Brown, *The Cross and Human Transformation: Paul's Apocalyptic Word in 1 Corinthians* (Minneapolis: Fortress, 1995), 97–139; André Munzinger, *Discerning the Spirits: Theological and Ethical Hermeneutics in Paul*, SNTSMS 140 (Cambridge: Cambridge University Press, 2007), 187, 194.

4. Munzinger, *Discerning the Spirits*, 68, 62.

5. Moyer Hubbard, "2 Corinthians," in Burke and Warrington, *Holy Spirit*, 166. So, in 11:4, in the course of a vigorous rhetorical contest with the "super-apostles" for the Corinthians' loyalty, Paul can speak disparagingly of a "different spirit" and "different gospel" to which the Corinthians have too easily submitted.

6. Gordon D. Fee highlights "Paul's firm conviction that the Spirit was both the *certain evidence* that the future had dawned, and the *absolute guarantee* of its final consummation" (*God's Empowering Presence* [Peabody, MA: Hendrickson, 1994; repr., Grand Rapids: Baker, 2011], 806; emphasis orig.).

8. The Holy Spirit in First Peter, Hebrews, and Revelation

1. For full development of the view that Revelation urges readers to re-sist cultural accommodation to the Roman Empire, see Warren Carter, *What Does Revelation Reveal? Unlocking the Mystery* (Nashville: Abing-don, 2011).

2. On the question of the author's identity, see M. Eugene Boring, *1 Peter*, ANTC (Nashville: Abingdon, 1999), 20–36; Lewis R. Donelson, *I & II Peter and Jude*, NTL (Louisville: Westminster John Knox, 2010), 15–17.

3. It offers "a home for the homeless," in the apt title of a work by John H. Elliott, *A Home for the Homeless: A Social-Scientific Criticism of 1 Peter, Its Situation and Strategy* (Minneapolis: Fortress, 1990; repr. Eugene, OR: Wipf and Stock, 2005).

4. The identity of these spirits is a much debated question in the inter-pretation of the letter. See Verena Schafroth, "1 and 2 Peter," in Burke and Warrington, *Holy Spirit*, 245–47; Donelson, *I & II Peter and Jude*, 112–17.

5. On the historical and cultural setting of Hebrews, see Craig R. Koester, *Hebrews: A New Translation and Commentary*, AB 36 (New Haven: Yale University Press, 2001), 64–78; Luke Timothy Johnson, *Hebrews: A Commentary*, NTL (Louisville: Westminster John Knox, 2006), 15–28, 32–38.

6. See Harold W. Attridge, *Hebrews: A Commentary on the Epistle to the Hebrews*, Hermeneia (Minneapolis: Fortress, 1989), 24.

7. Levison argues that the Spirit "testifies" (present tense) not in the past composition of scriptural texts but precisely by interpreting them within the context of the living community being addressed by the author (Levison, *Inspired*, 154–62, esp. 156).

8. On the setting and circumstance of Revelation, see Brian K. Blount, *Revelation: A Commentary*, NTL (Louisville: Westminster John Knox, 2009), 8–14; M. Eugene Boring, *Revelation*, IBC (Louisville: West-minster John Knox, 1989), 5–23; Mitchell G. Reddish, *Revelation*,

SHBC (Macon, GA: Smyth and Helwys, 2001), 7–17; Adela Yarbro Collins, *Crisis and Catharsis: The Power of the Apocalypse* (Philadelphia: Westminster, 1984), 84–110.

9. Richard Bauckham, "The Role of the Spirit," in *The Climax of Prophecy*, ed. Richard Bauckham (London: T and T Clark, 1993), 150; Levison, *Inspired*, 86–87.

10. See Blount, *Revelation*, 31, 33, 91, 412; Reddish, *Revelation*, 35.

11. Bauckham, "The Role of the Spirit," 158; emphasis added.

12. Ibid., 153.

13. Ibid., 166.

14. Ibid., 166–67.

15. John Christopher Thomas, "Revelation," in Burke and Warrington, *Holy Spirit*, 264.

9. Trajectories and Themes

1. Colin Gunton, *The Promise of Trinitarian Theology*, 2nd ed. (Edinburgh: T and T Clark, 1997), xv, quoted in Beverly R. Gaventa, "Pentecost and Trinity," *Int* 66 (2012): 11.

2. The bibliography for this chapter lists representative works from these authors. See also the extremely helpful anthology of judiciously chosen (brief) excerpts gathered in Veli-Matti Kärkkäinen, ed., *Holy Spirit and Salvation: The Sources of Christian Theology* (Louisville: Westminster John Knox, 2010); the critical engagement with a variety of authors in Anthony C. Thiselton, *Holy Spirit*, and ibid., *A Shorter Guide to the Holy Spirit: Bible, Doctrine, Experience* (Grand Rapids: Eerdmans, 2016); and the many incisive contributions of John R. Levison (e.g., recently, *Inspired: The Holy Spirit and the Mind of Faith*).

3. Kärkkäinen, *Holy Spirit and Salvation*, 363–71, 398–457; Thiselton, *Shorter Guide*, 137–90; Amos Yong, *The Spirit Poured Out on All Flesh:*

Pentecostalism and the Possibility of Global Theology (Grand Rapids: Baker, 2005).

4. See the vigorous development of this view in Levison, *Inspired*.

5. Ibid., 185.

6. Ibid.

7. Ibid., 226, 222.

8. E.g., C. K. Barrett, *The Holy Spirit and the Gospel Tradition* (London: SPCK, 1947), 108–9.

Subject Index

Scripture Index

Made in United States
Troutdale, OR
02/27/2024

18010930R00119